Balance Benders™
Level 2

Series Titles
Balance Benders™
Beginning ▪ Level 1▪ Level 2 ▪ Level 3

Written by
Robert Femiano

Graphic Design by
Karla Garrett ▪ Annette Langenstein ▪ Trisha Dreyer

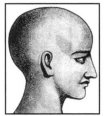

© 2010
THE CRITICAL THINKING CO.™
www.CriticalThinking.com
Phone: 800-458-4849 • Fax: 831-393-3277
P.O. Box 1610 • Seaside • CA 93955-1610
ISBN 978-1-60144-227-7

Mixed Sources
Product group from well-managed
forests and other controlled sources
www.fsc.org Cert no. SW-COC-002283
© 1996 Forest Stewardship Council

TABLE OF CONTENTS

The Value of This Book

Move over Sudoku, here come *Balance Benders*™! You can use these books as quick, fun, logic problems or as stepping-stones to success in algebra. Students develop deductive thinking and pre-algebra skills as they solve balance puzzles that are more fun and addictive than Sudoku puzzles! Students must analyze each balance to identify the clues, and then synthesize the information to solve the puzzle. Try one—and then try to stop!

Teaching Suggestions

The solution to each puzzle in this book involves one or more of the algebraic thinking concepts on pages 38-39. After you work through a few puzzles with the student, read and discuss these 10 Balance Tips with the student to make sure he is familiar with all of them. Developing these essential skills used in balancing and solving equations has never been more fun!

A student might occasionally be stumped by a puzzle so an upside-down hint is provided below each puzzle.

It often helps to remind students that the joy of puzzles is being puzzled. Do your best to keep them fun and remember that it is just as important to praise perseverance as it is to praise the correct answer.

About the Author

A longtime puzzle fan, Robert Femiano is a Seattle public school elementary educator and has been for most of his 34-year teaching career. For more than a decade of this time, he was also adjunct faculty at Seattle Pacific University conducting math methods courses. Publications include *Algebraic Problem Solving in the Primary Grades* in the National Council for Teachers of Mathematics peer-reviewed journal and *Quick Thinks Math* books and software by The Critical Thinking Co.™. In 2002, he won the highest honor in education, the Presidential Award for Excellence in Mathematics and Science Teaching.

Which answer can replace the question mark?

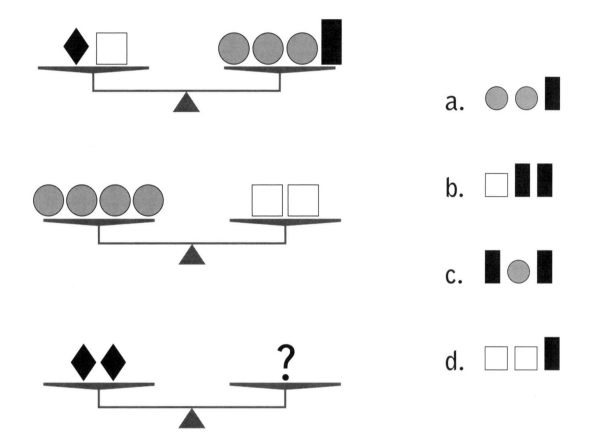

a.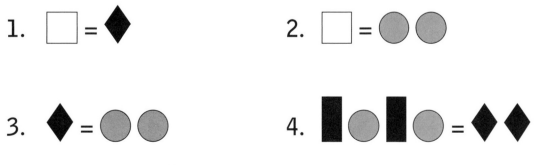

b.

c.

d.

Circle the two answers below that will always be true.

1. ☐ = ◆   2. ☐ = ⬤⬤

3. ◆ = ⬤⬤   4. ▮⬤▮⬤ = ◆◆

Hint: Divide 2nd balance in half.

1

Which answer can replace the question mark?

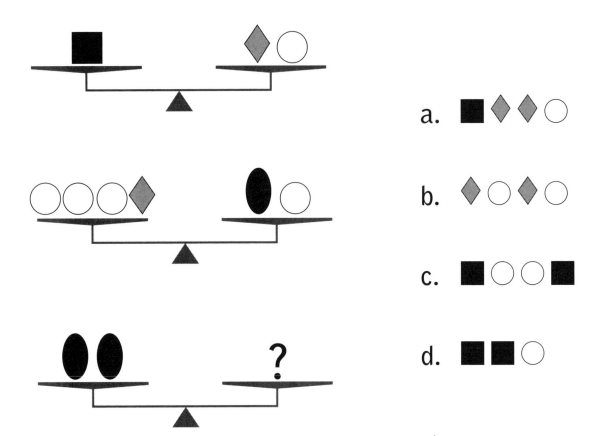

a.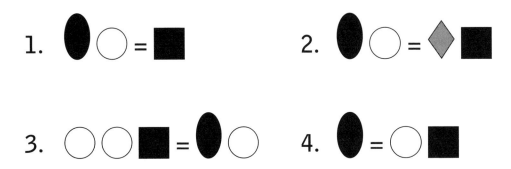

b.

c.

d.

Circle the two answers below that will always be true.

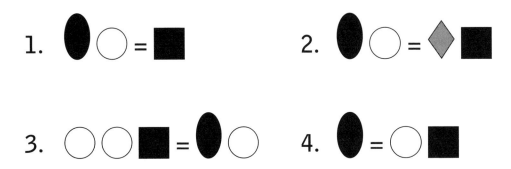

1. ⬤ ◯ = ⬛

2. ⬤ ◯ = ◆ ⬛

3. ◯ ◯ ⬛ = ⬤ ◯

4. ⬤ = ◯ ⬛

Hint: From 1st balance, substitute ⬛ for ◆ ⬤ on 2nd balance.

Which answer can replace the question mark?

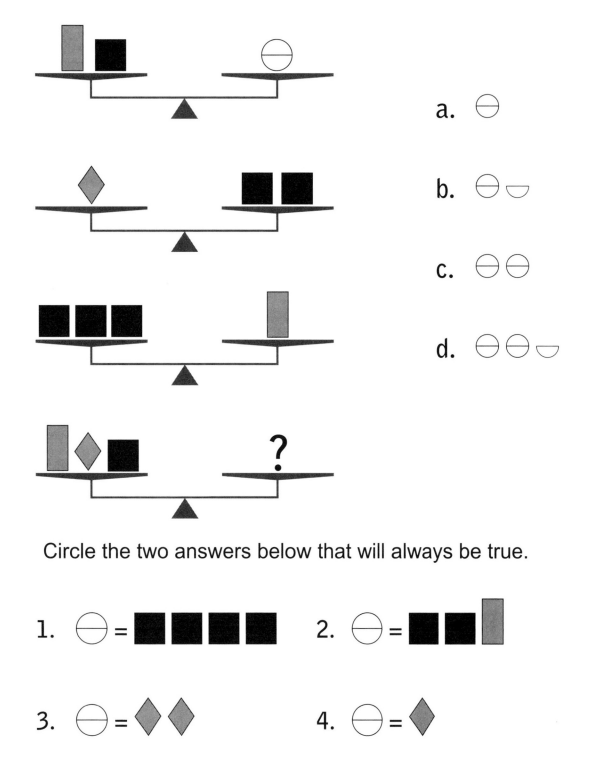

Circle the two answers below that will always be true.

Hint: From 3rd balance, substitute ■ ■ for ▮ on 1st balance.

Which answer can replace the question mark?

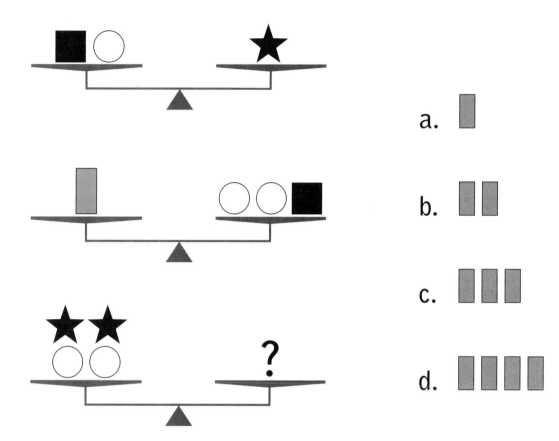

Circle the two answers below that will always be true.

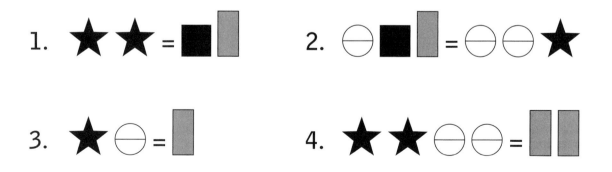

Which answer can replace the question mark?

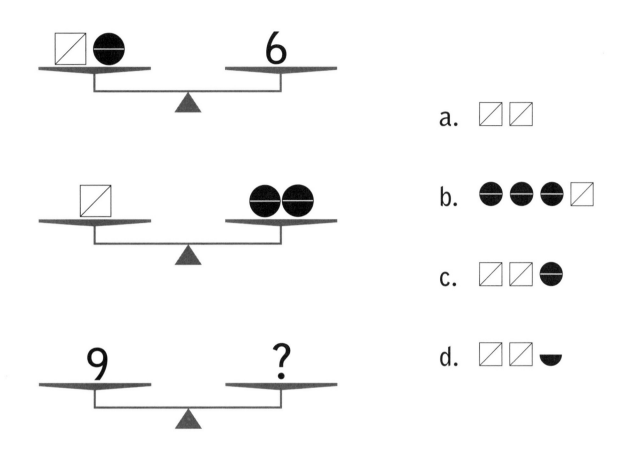

a. ▱▱

b. ⬤⬤⬤▱

c. ▱▱⬤

d. ▱▱◗

Circle the two answers below that will always be true.

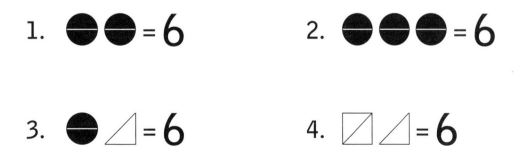

Which answer can replace the question mark?

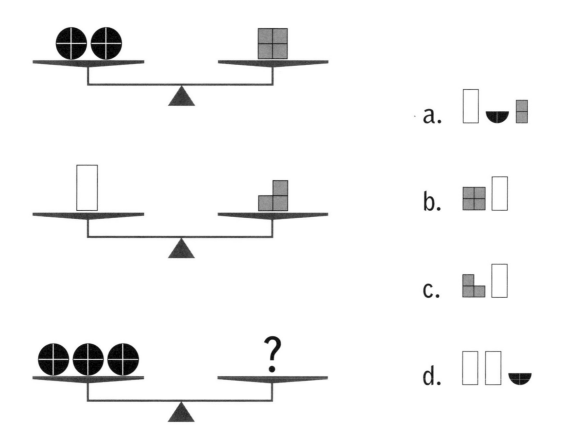

Circle the two answers below that will always be true.

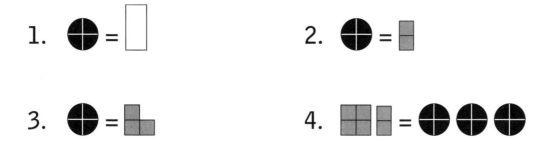

Hint: Divide 1st balance in half.

Which answer can replace the question mark?

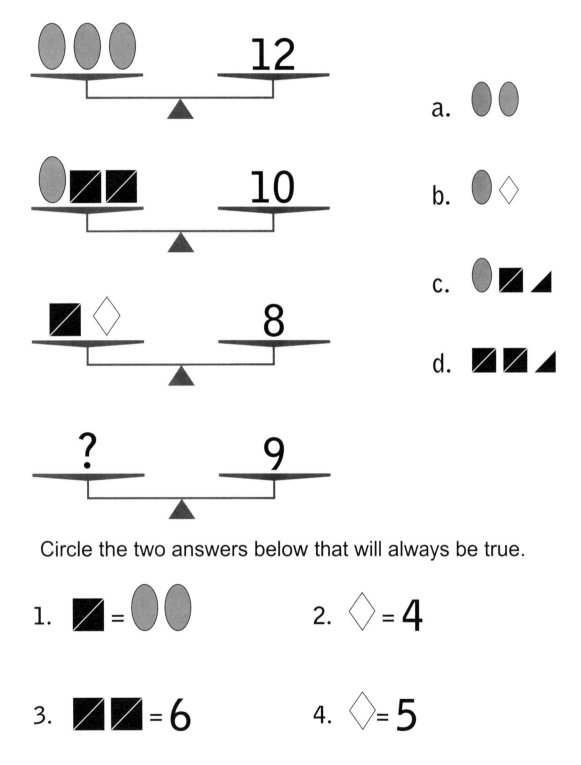

Circle the two answers below that will always be true.

Hint: Divide 1st balance in thirds.

Which answer can replace the question mark?

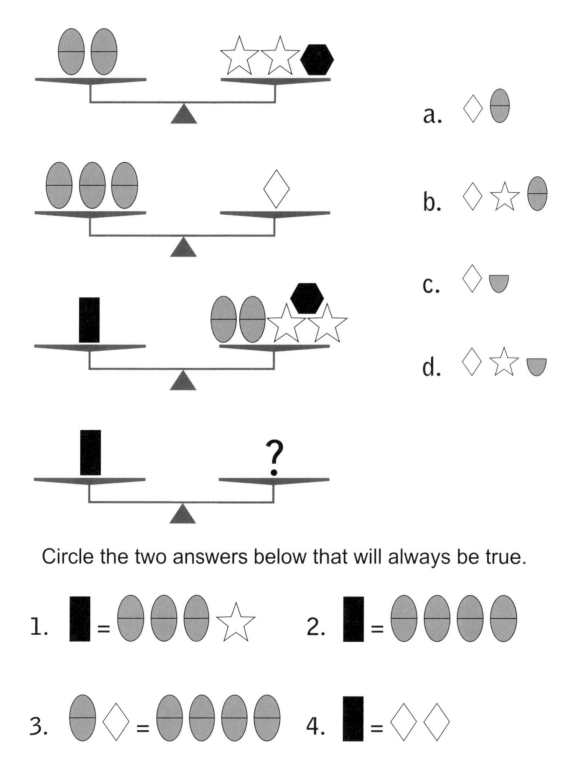

Circle the two answers below that will always be true.

Hint: From 1st balance, substitute ⬭⬭ for ☆ ☆ on 3rd balance.

Which answer can replace the question mark?

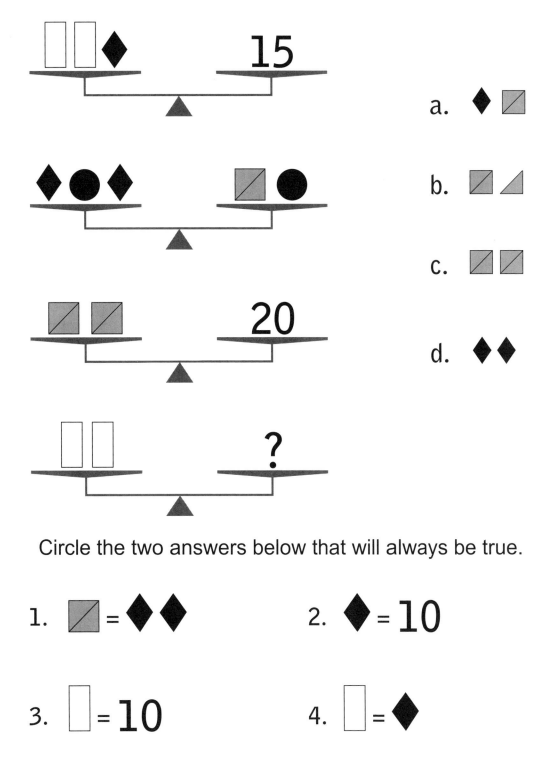

Circle the two answers below that will always be true.

Hint: On 2nd balance, remove ● from both pans.

Which answer can replace the question mark?

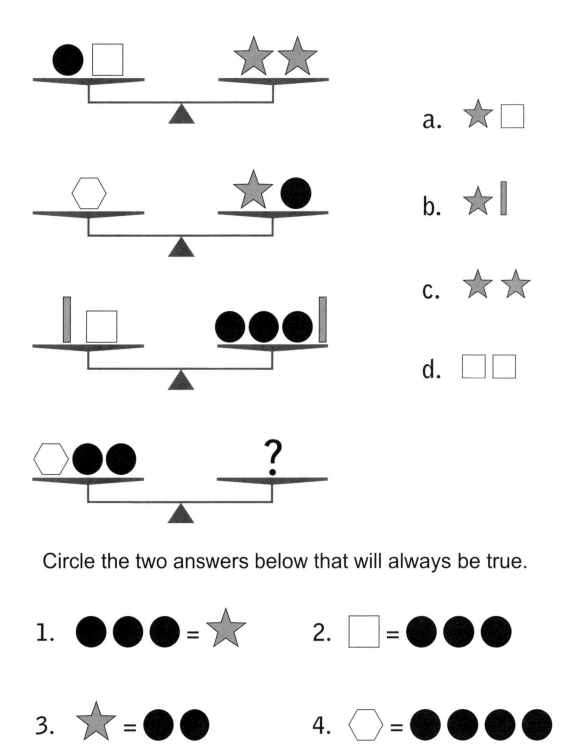

Circle the two answers below that will always be true.

Hint: On 3rd balance, remove ‖ from both pans.

Which answer can replace the question mark?

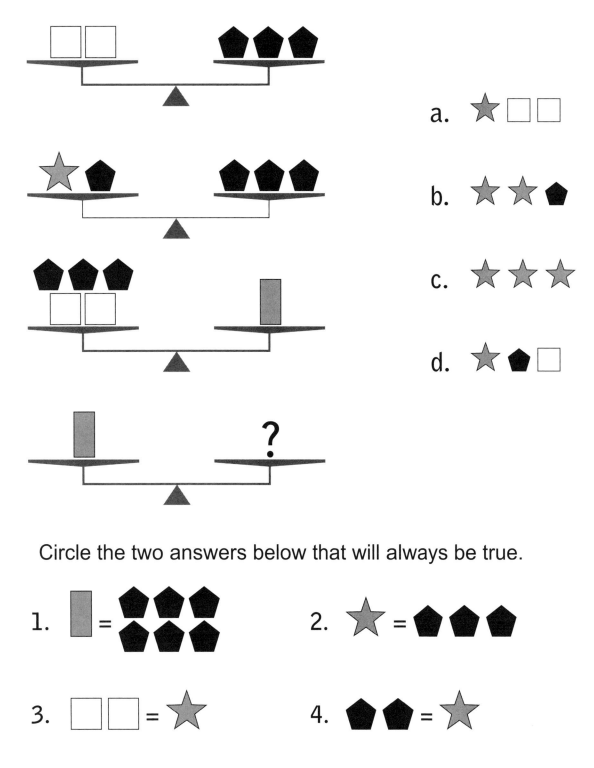

Circle the two answers below that will always be true.

Hint: From 1st balance, substitute ● ● for □□ on 3rd balance.

Which answer can replace the question mark?

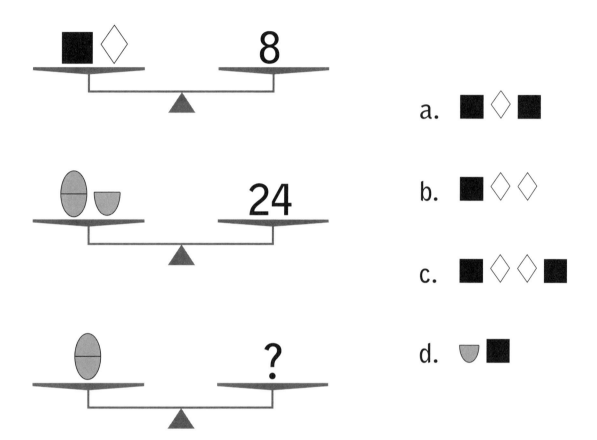

Circle the two answers below that will always be true.

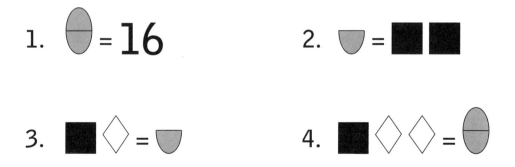

Hint: Divide 2nd balance in thirds.

Which answer can replace the question mark?

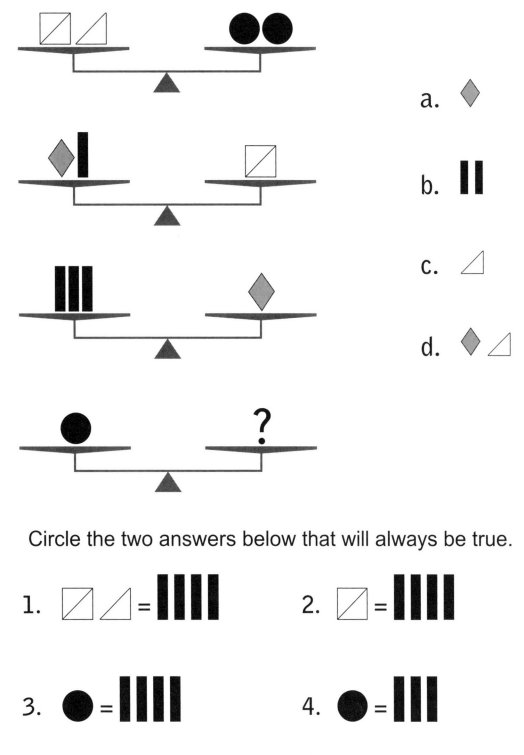

Which answer can replace the question mark?

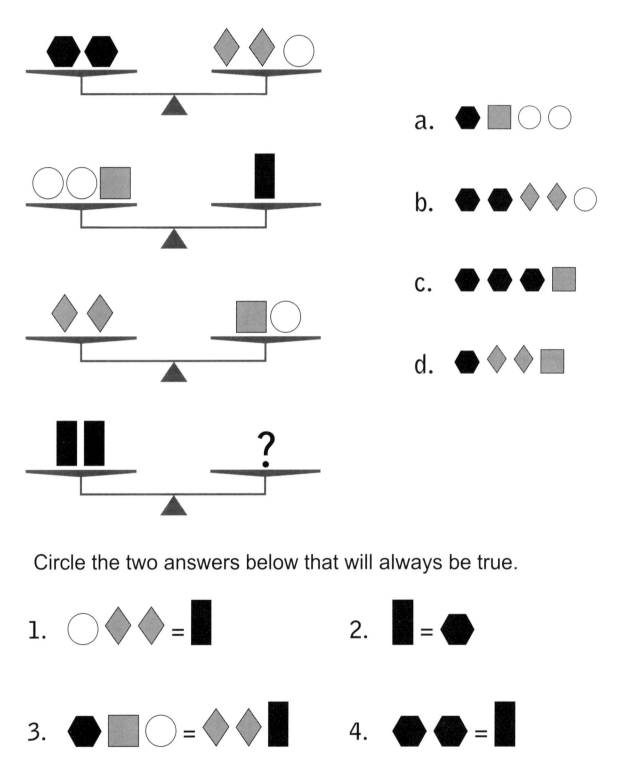

Circle the two answers below that will always be true.

Which answer can replace the question mark?

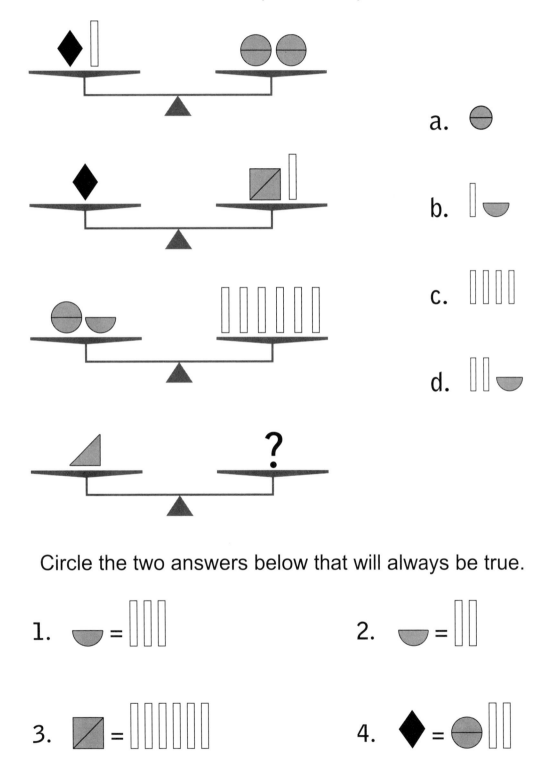

Circle the two answers below that will always be true.

Which answer can replace the question mark?

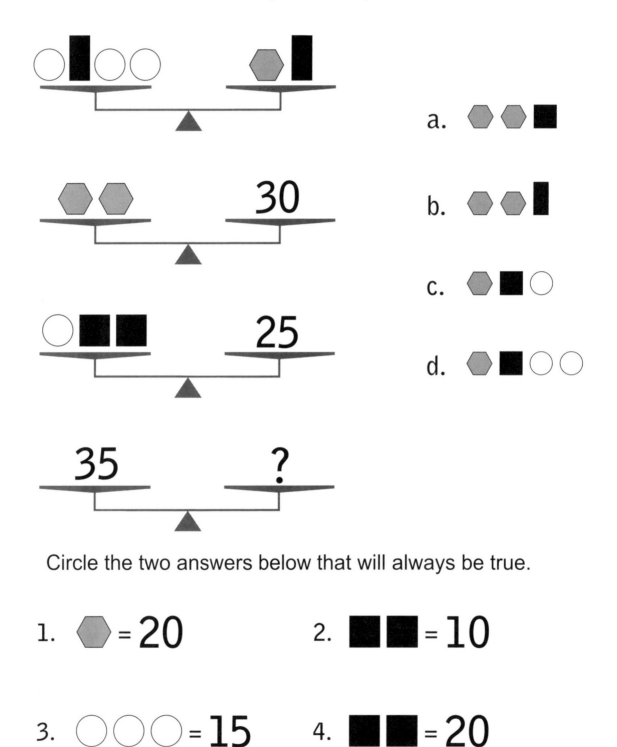

Circle the two answers below that will always be true.

Which answer can replace the question mark?

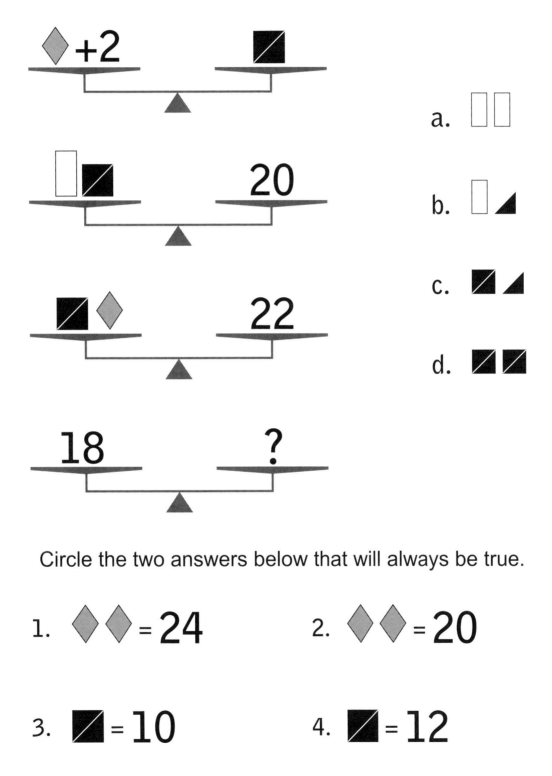

Circle the two answers below that will always be true.

1. ◆◆ = 24   2. ◆◆ = 20

3. ◼ = 10   4. ◼ = 12

Hint: From 1st balance, substitute ◆ + 2 for ◼ on 3rd balance.

Which answer can replace the question mark?

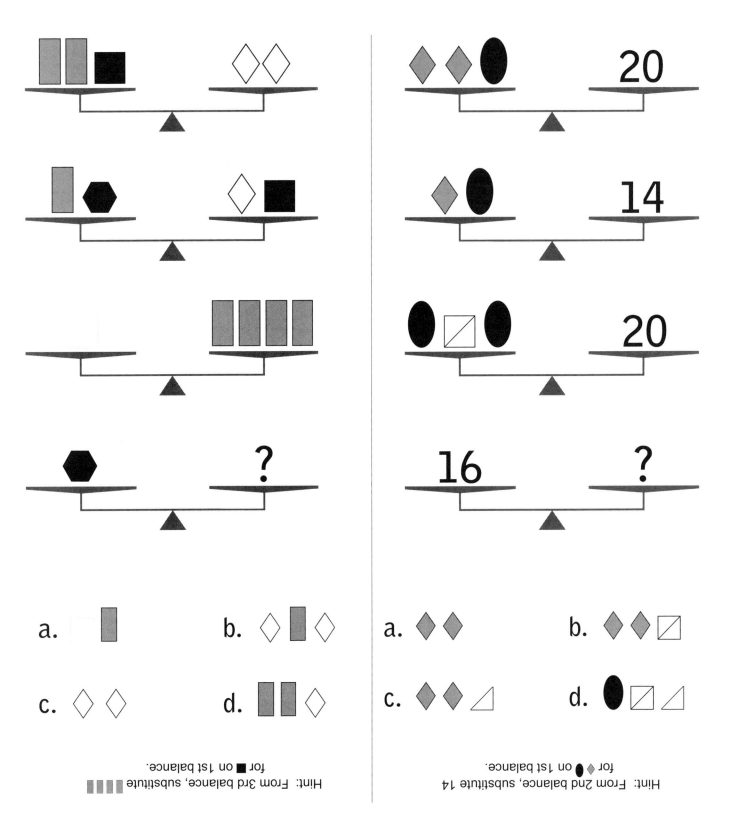

Which answer can replace the question mark?

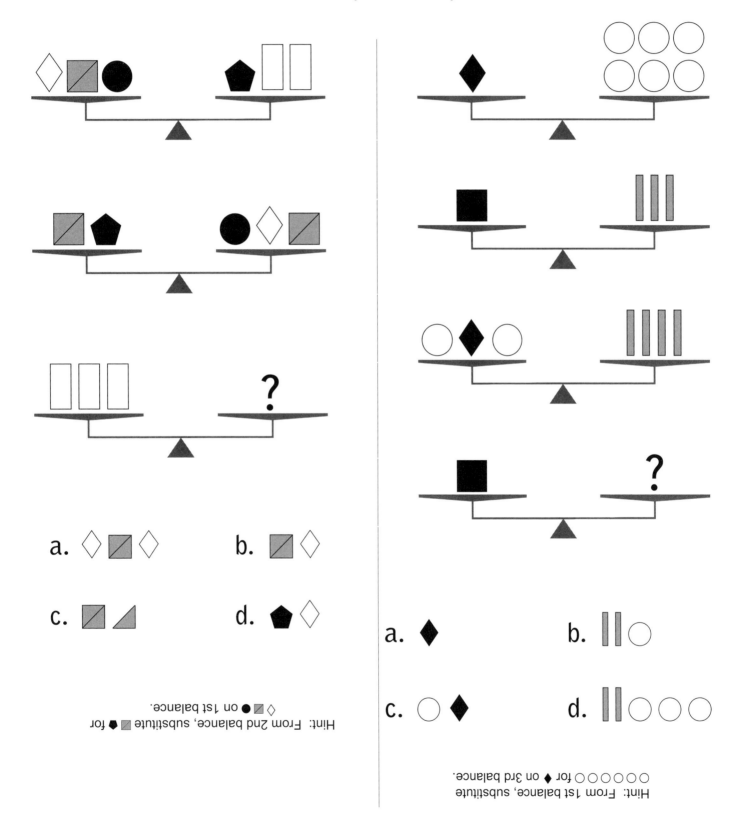

a. ◇ ◩ ◇   b. ◩ ◇

c. ◩ ◸   d. ⬠ ◇

Hint: From 2nd balance, substitute ◩ for ⬠
◇ ◩ ● on 1st balance.

a. ◆   b. ‖ ○

c. ○ ◆   d. ‖ ○ ○ ○

Hint: From 1st balance, substitute
○ ○ ○ ○ ○ for ◆ on 3rd balance.

Balance Benders™

Which answer can replace the question mark?

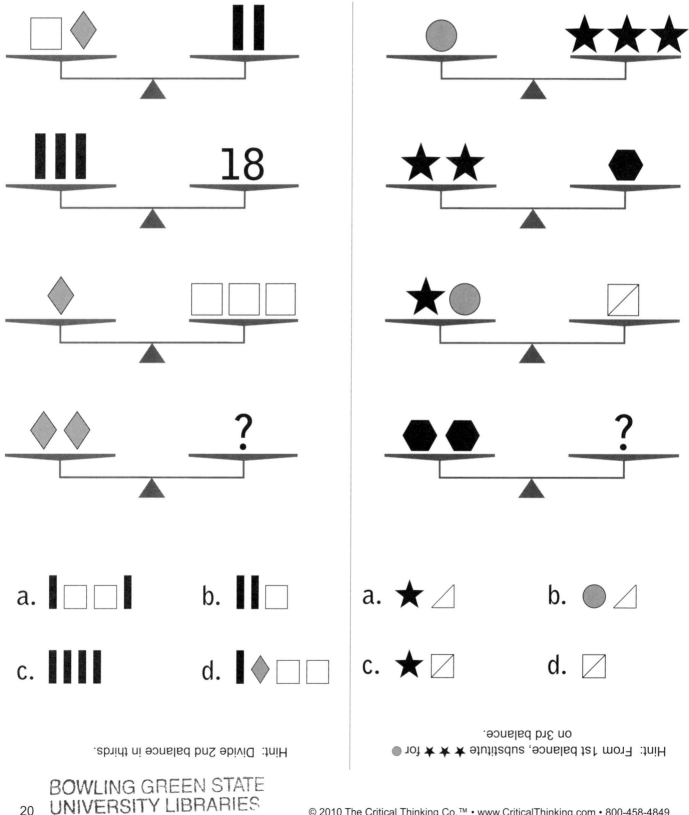

a. ▌☐☐▌   b. ▌▌☐

c. ▌▌▌▌   d. ▌◆☐☐

a. ★◁   b. ⬤◁

c. ★▱   d. ▱

Hint: Divide 2nd balance in thirds.

Hint: From 1st balance, substitute ★ ★ ★ for ⬤ on 3rd balance.

Which answer can replace the question mark?

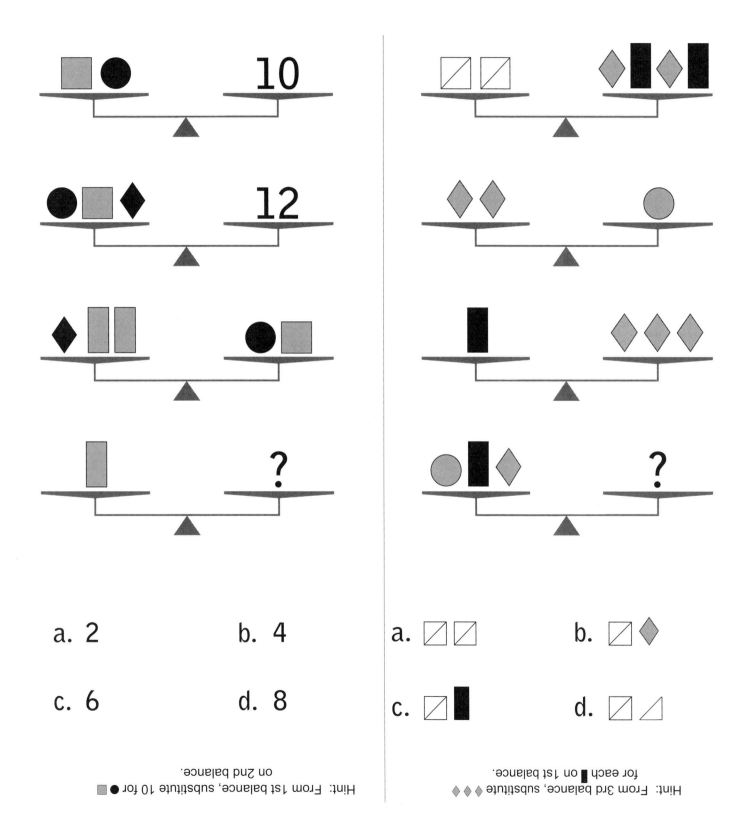

a. 2   b. 4

c. 6   d. 8

a. ▨ ▨   b. ▨ ◆

c. ▨ ▮   d. ▨ ◹

Hint: From 1st balance, substitute 10 for ▨ ●
on 2nd balance.

Hint: From 3rd balance, substitute ◆ ◆ ◆
for each ▮ on 1st balance.

Which answer can replace the question mark?

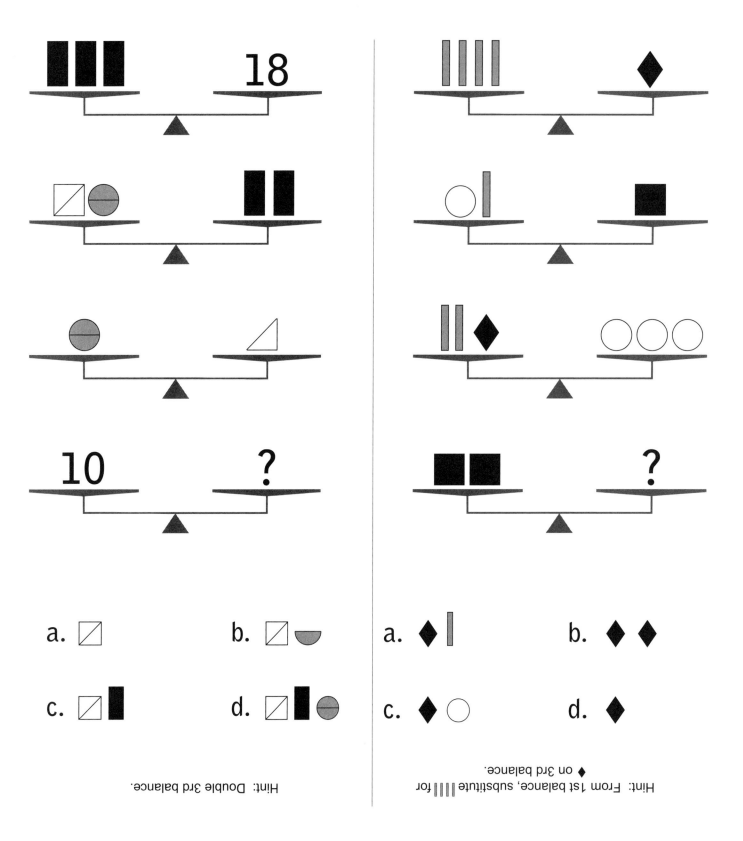

Which answer can replace the question mark?

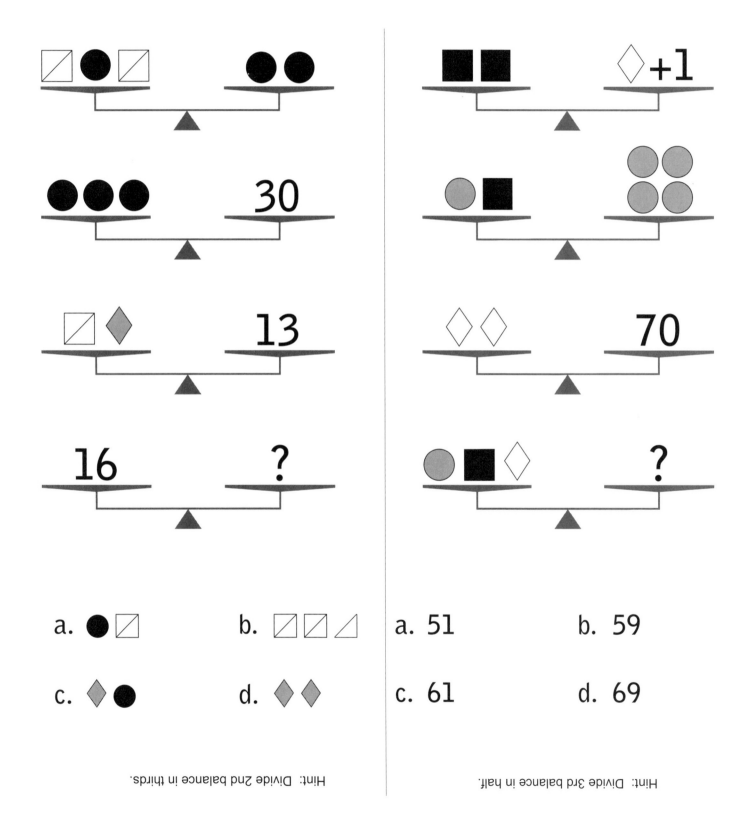

a. ● ◻

b. ◻ ◻ ◿

c. ◆ ●

d. ◆ ◆

a. 51

b. 59

c. 61

d. 69

Hint: Divide 2nd balance in thirds.

Hint: Divide 3rd balance in half.

Which answer can replace the question mark?

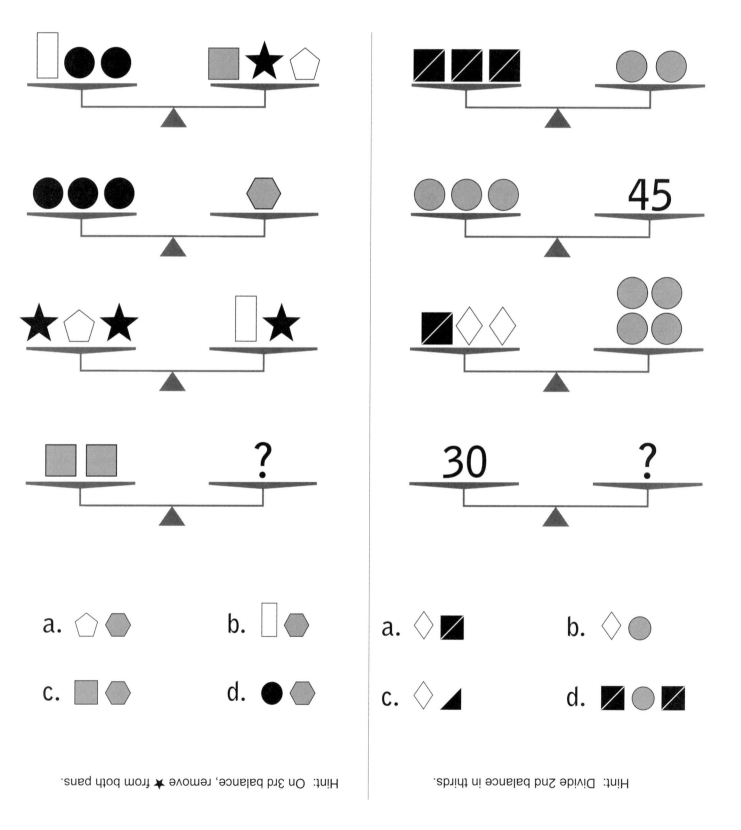

Which answer can replace the question mark?

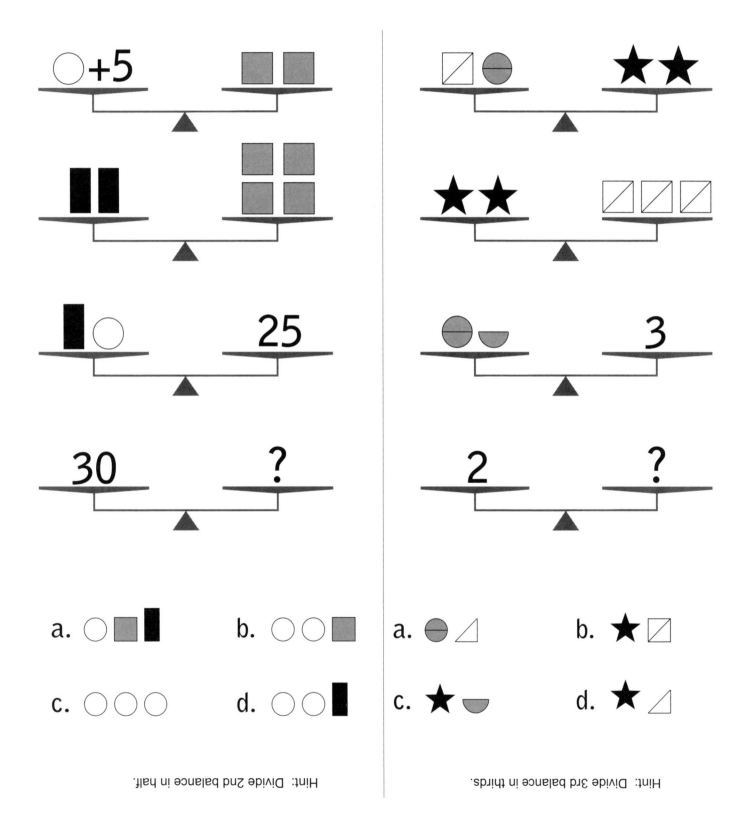

Which answer can replace the question mark?

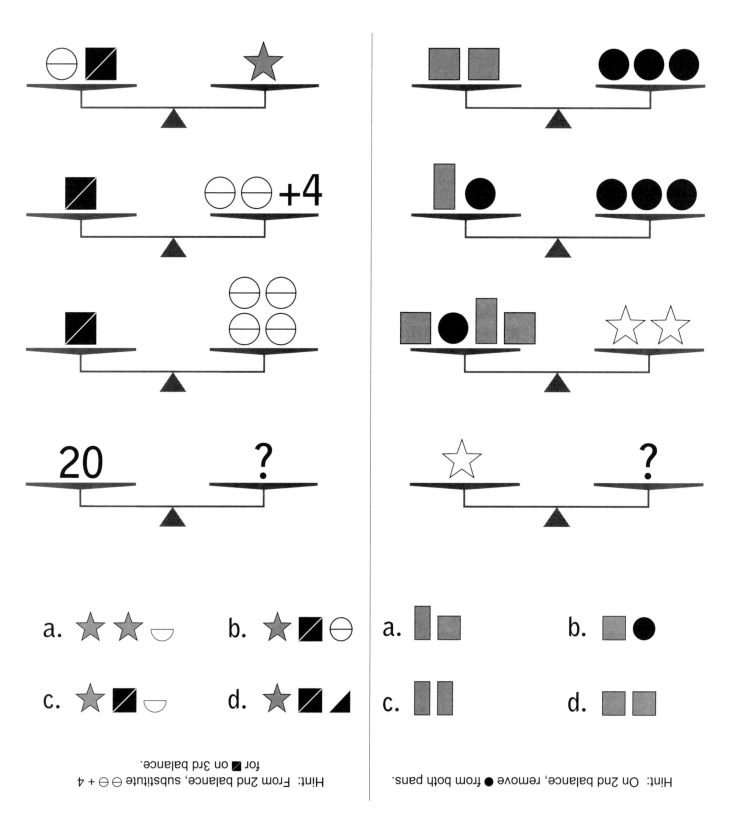

Which answer can replace the question mark?

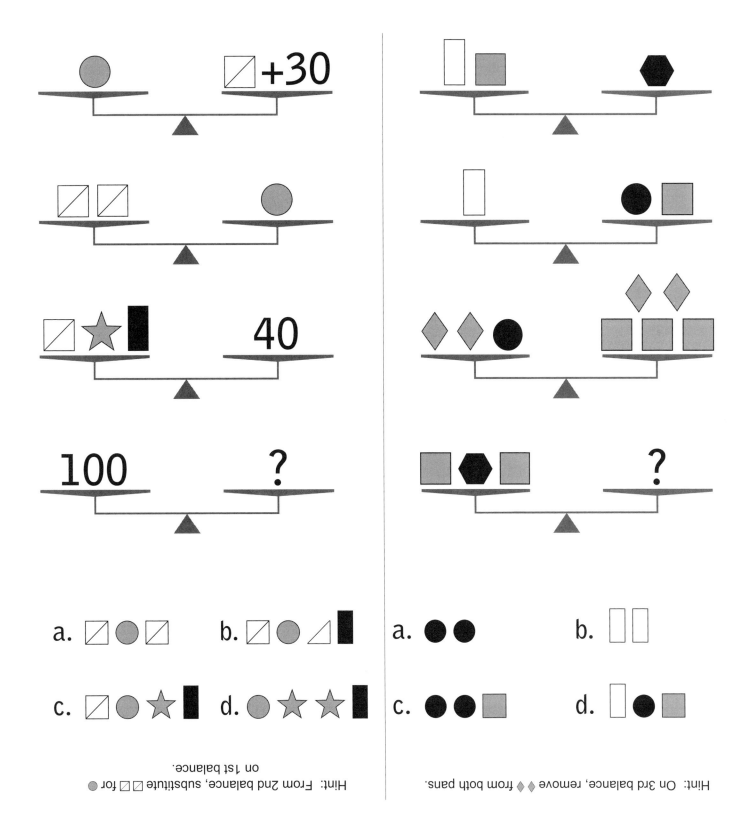

a. ▨ ⬤ ▨   b. ▨ ⬤ ◹ ▮

c. ▨ ⬤ ★ ▮   d. ⬤ ★ ★ ▮

a. ⬤ ⬤   b. ▯ ▯

c. ⬤ ⬤ ▢   d. ▯ ⬤ ▢

Hint: From 2nd balance, substitute ▨▨ for ⬤ on 1st balance.

Hint: On 3rd balance, remove ◆ ◆ from both pans.

Which answer can replace the question mark?

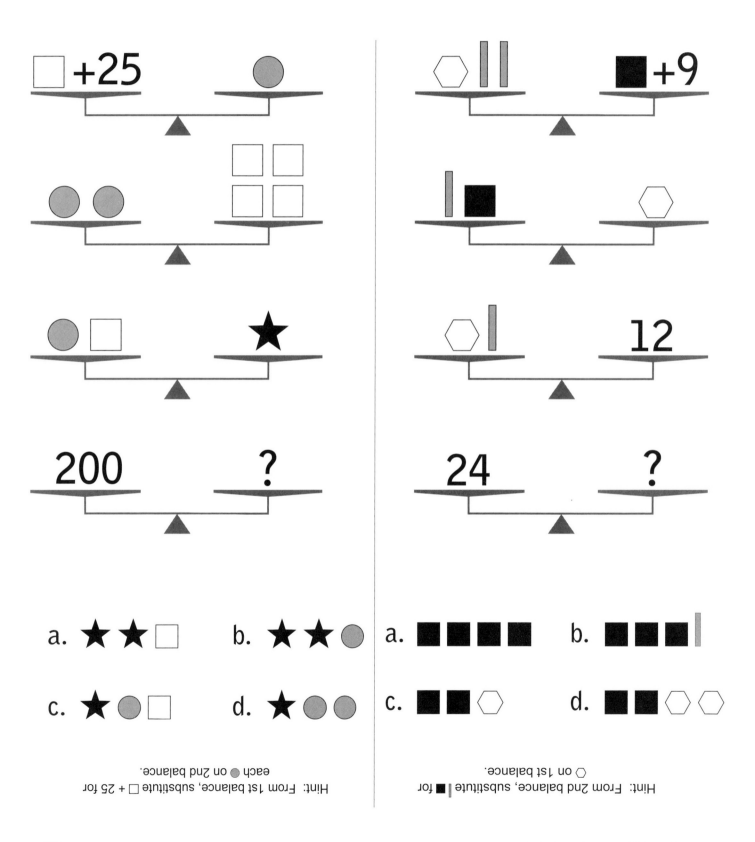

Which answer can replace the question mark?

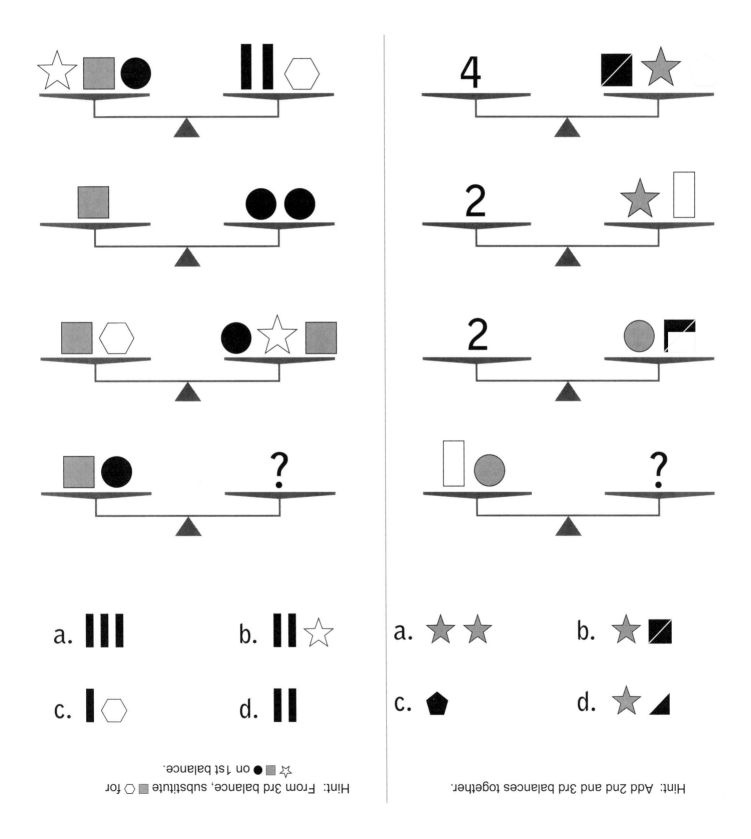

Which answer can replace the question mark?

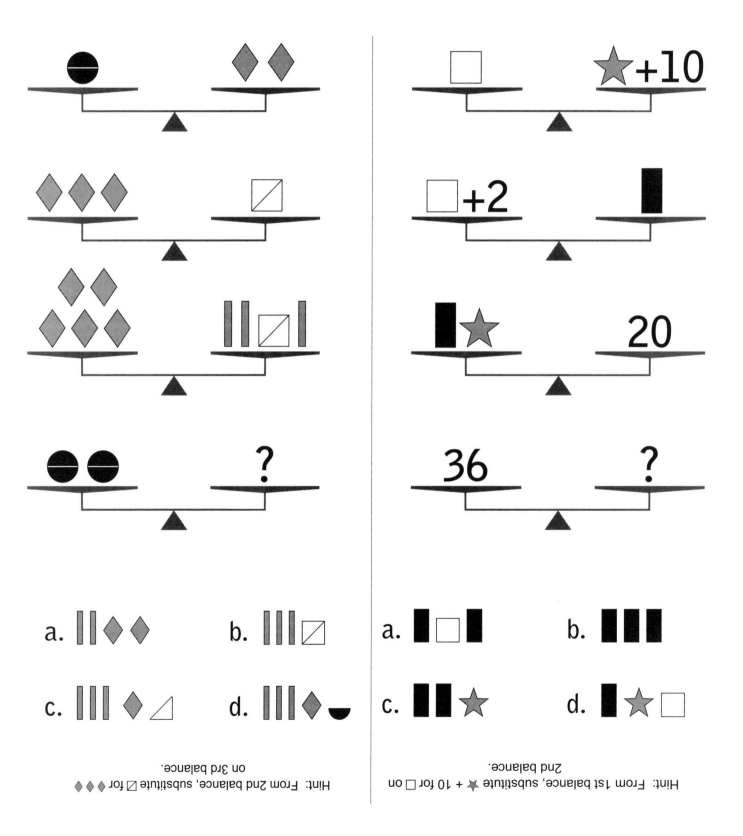

a. ∥ ◆ ◆   b. ∥∥ ◻

c. ∥∥ ◆ △   d. ∥∥ ◆ ⌣

a. ▮ ◻ ▮   b. ▮ ▮ ▮

c. ▮ ▮ ★   d. ▮ ★ ◻

Hint: From 2nd balance, substitute ◻ for ◆ ◆ ◆ on 3rd balance.

Hint: From 1st balance, substitute ★ + 10 for ◻ on 2nd balance.

Which answer can replace the question mark?

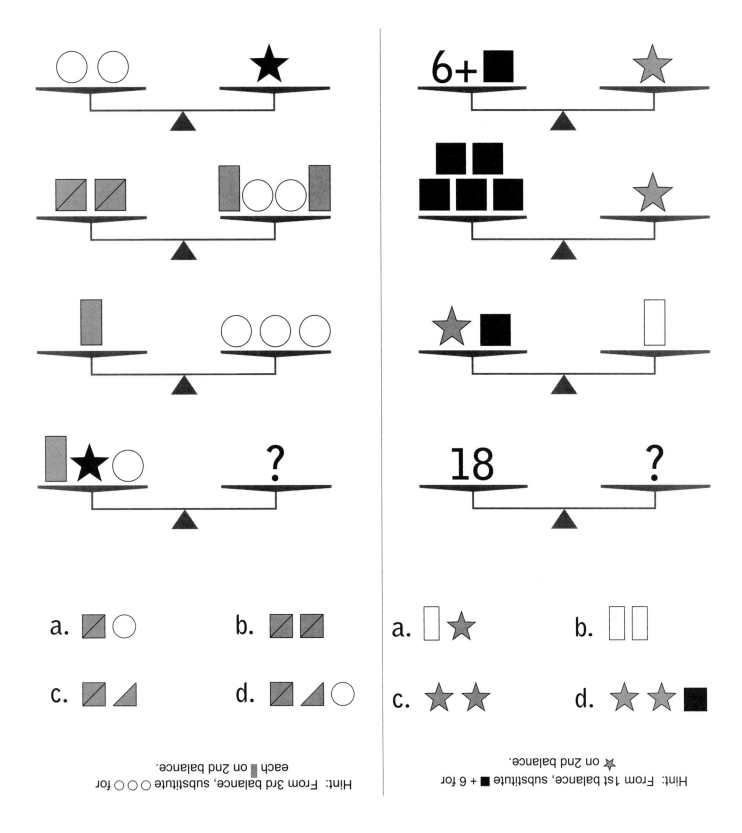

Which answer can replace the question mark?

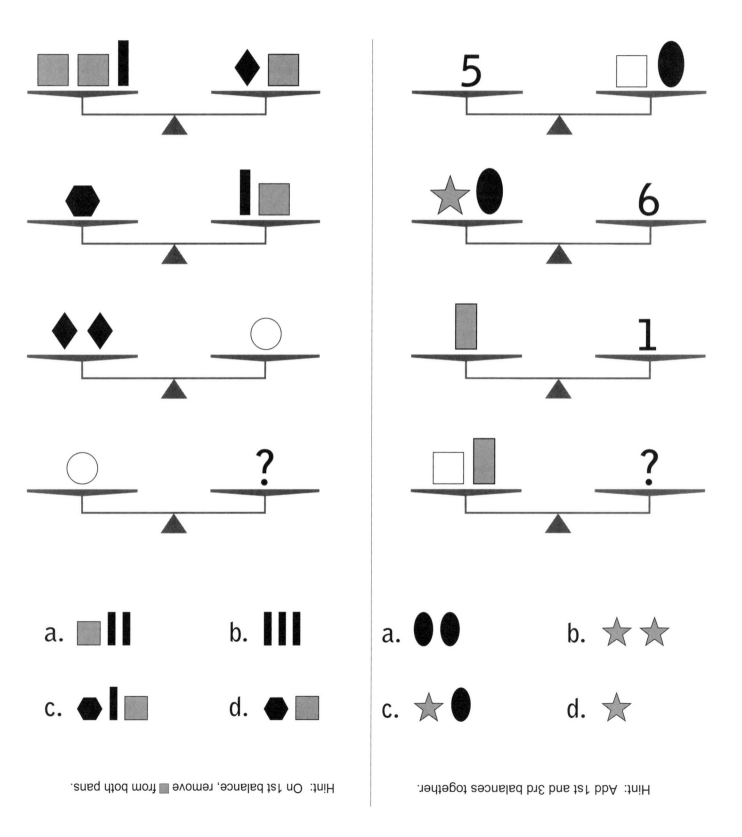

Which answer can replace the question mark?

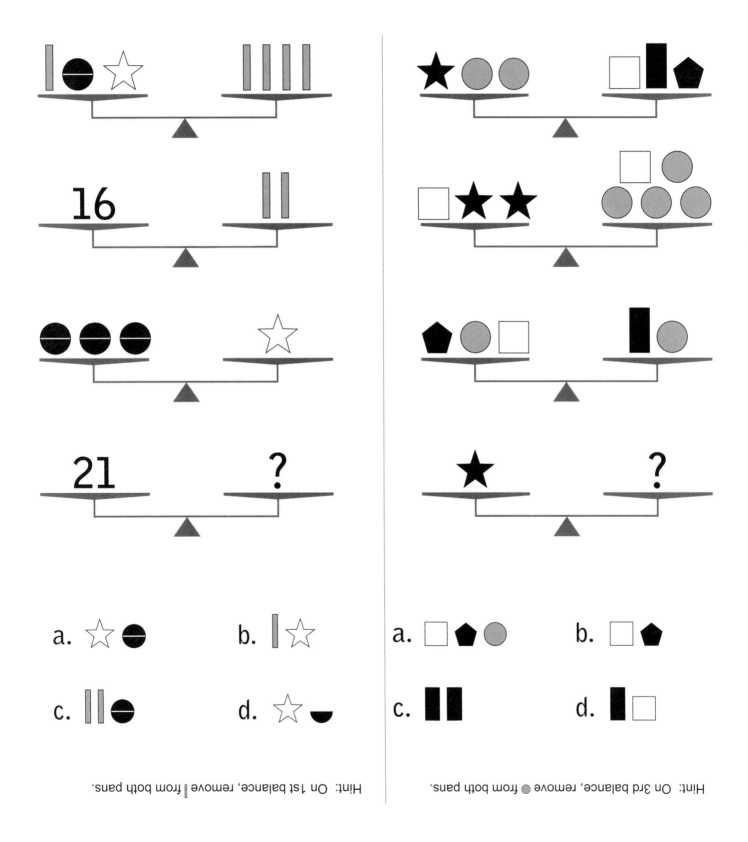

Which answer can replace the question mark?

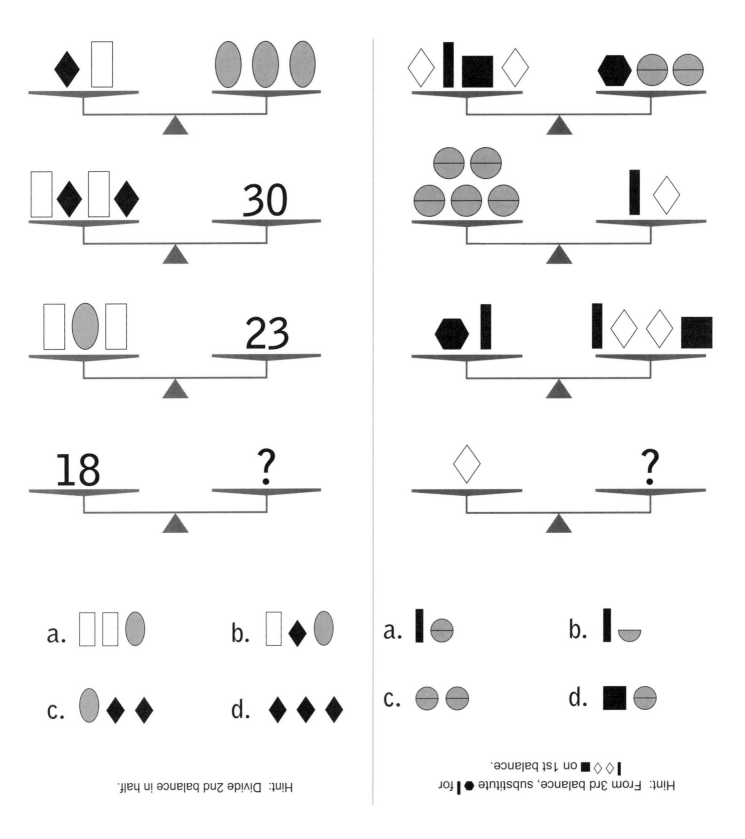

Which answer can replace the question mark?

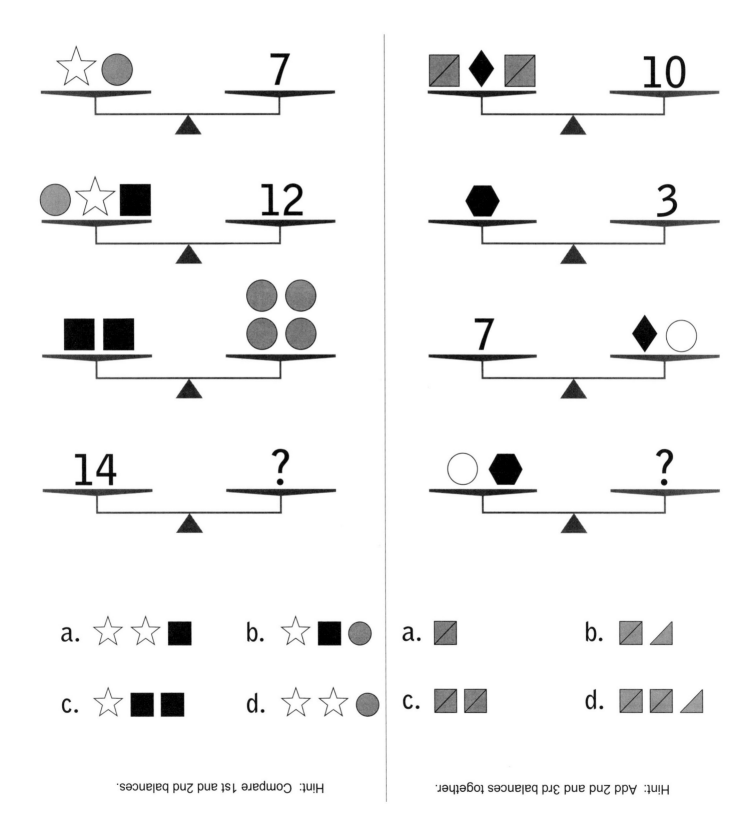

Hint: Compare 1st and 2nd balances.

Hint: Add 2nd and 3rd balances together.

Which answer can replace the question mark?

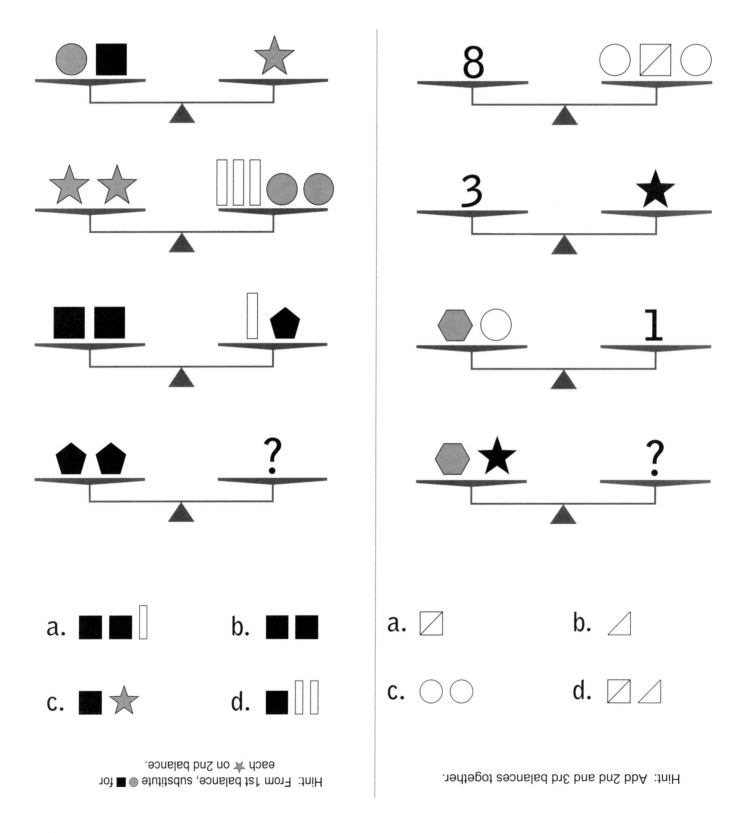

a. ■ ■ ▯   b. ■ ■

c. ■ ★   d. ■ ▯▯

a. ◻   b. ◺

c. ○ ○   d. ◻ ◺

Which answer can replace the question mark?

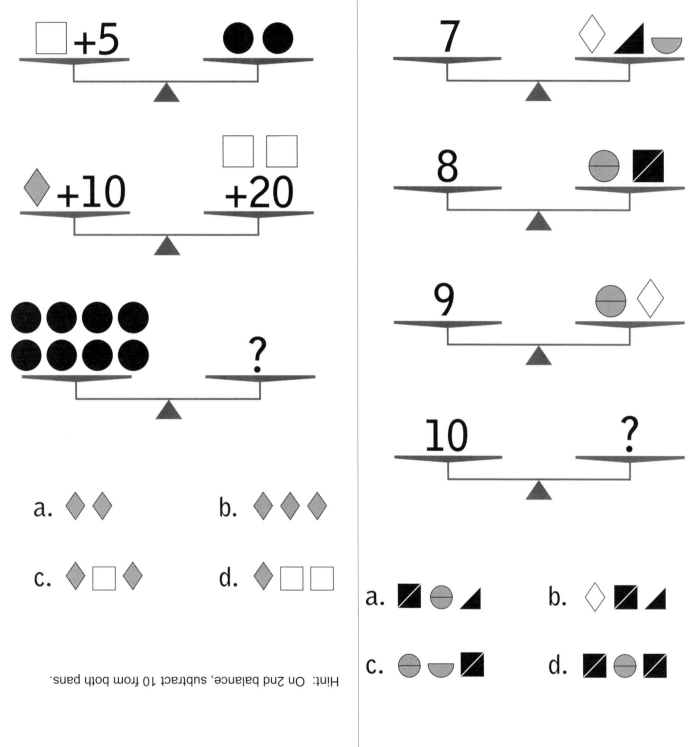

BALANCE TIPS
(ALGEBRA CONCEPTS)

1. Reversing the pans does not change the balance of
    the scale. For example . . .

    If a = b then b = a
    If a > b then b < a

    Symmetric Property of Equality and Inequality

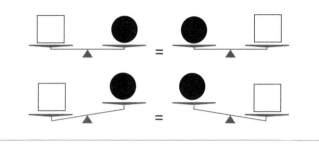

2. Rearranging "weights" does not change the balance of
    the scale. For example . . .

    a + b = b + a
    If a + b < c then b + a < c
    If a + b > c then b + a > c

    Commutative Property of Equality and Inequality

    a + (b + c) = (a + b) + c

    Associative Property of Equality and Inequality

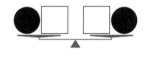

3. Adding the same "weight" to each pan does not change
    the balance of the scale. For example . . .

    If a = b then a + c = b + c
    If a < b then a + c < b + c
    If a > b then a + c > b + c

    Addition Property of Equality and Inequality

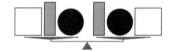

If   then

4. Subtracting the same "weight" from each pan does not
    change the balance of the scale. For example . . .

    If a = b then a - c = b - c
    If a < b then a - c < b - c
    If a > b then a - c > b - c

    Subtraction Property of Equality and Inequality

If   then

5. Multiplying both pans equally (e.g. doubling) does not
    change the balance of the scale. For example . . .

    If a = b then a ∗ c = b ∗ c
    If a < b then a ∗ c < b ∗ c
    If a > b then a ∗ c > b ∗ c

    Multiplication Property of Equality and Inequality

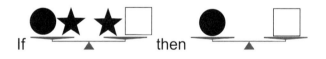

If   then

BALANCE TIPS (Cont.)
(ALGEBRA CONCEPTS)

6. Dividing or partitioning both pans into equally numbered groups (e.g. take half) does not change the balance of the scale. For example . . .

   If a = b then a/c = b/c
   If a < b then a/c < b/c
   If a > b then a/c > b/c

   Division Property of Equality and Inequality

7. Substitute one "weight" for a similar "weight" or group of "weights." For example . . .

   If a = b then "a" can be substituted for "b" in any equation or inequality

   Substitution Property of Equality and Inequality

   If a = b and b = c then a = c
   If a < b and b < c then a < c
   If a > b and b > c then a > c

   Transitive Property of Equality and Inequality

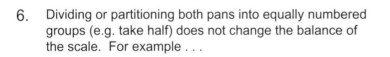

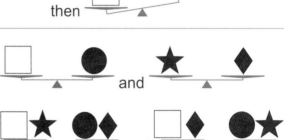

8. Combining two balanced scales does not change the balance of the new scale. For example . . .

   If a = b and c = d then a + c = b + d and a + d = b + c

   Addition and Substitution Properties

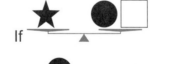

9. Removing a "weight" from one pan of a balanced scale causes an imbalance. For example . . .

   If a + b = c then c > a and c > b

   Equation to Inequality or Trichotomy Property

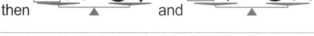

10. When multiplying or dividing, be sure to do the same to all "weights" in the pans. For example . . .

    a * (b + c) = (a * b) + (a * c)

    Distributive Property

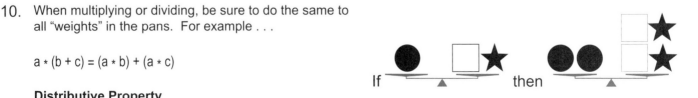

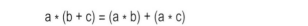

Solutions

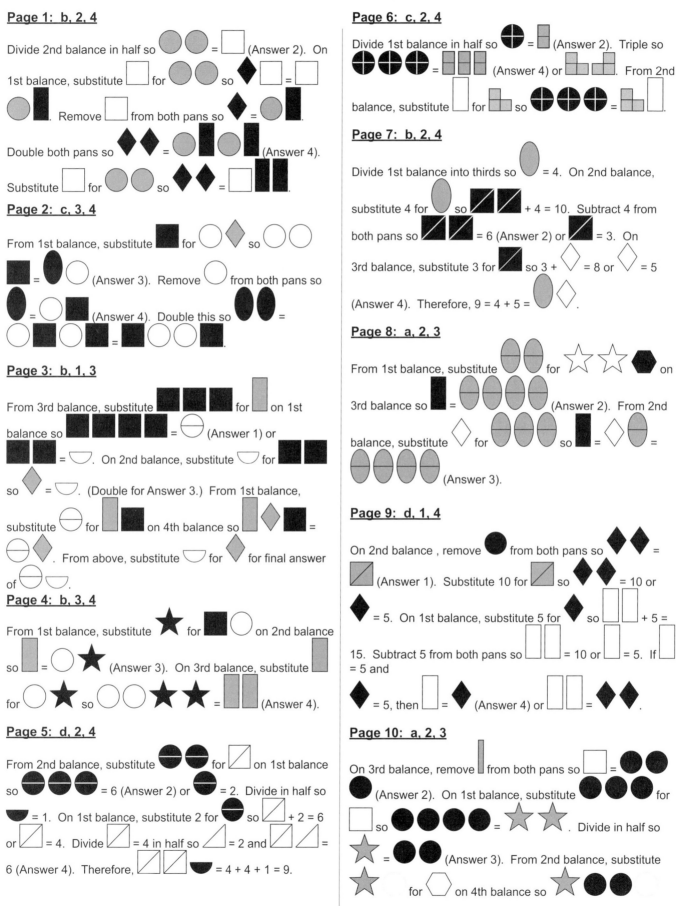

Page 1: b, 2, 4

Divide 2nd balance in half so ⬤⬤ = ☐ (Answer 2). On 1st balance, substitute ☐ for ⬤⬤ so ◆ ☐ = ☐. ⬤ ▮. Remove ☐ from both pans so ◆ = ▮.

Double both pans so ◆◆ = ⬤ ▮ (Answer 4). Substitute ☐ for ⬤⬤ so ◆◆ = ☐ ▮▮.

Page 2: c, 3, 4

From 1st balance, substitute ▪ for ⬭◇ so ◯◯ ▪ = ⬭ ◯ (Answer 3). Remove ◯ from both pans so ⬭ ▪ = ◯ (Answer 4). Double this so ⬭⬭ = ◯ ▪ ◯ ▪ = ◯ ▪ ◯ ◯ ▪.

Page 3: b, 1, 3

From 3rd balance, substitute ▪▪▪ for ▮ on 1st balance so ▪▪▪▪▪ = ◯ (Answer 1) or ▪▪ = ◡. On 2nd balance, substitute ◡ for ▪▪ so ◆ = ◡. (Double for Answer 3.) From 1st balance, substitute ◡ for ▮ on 4th balance so ▮ ◆ ▪ = ◯ ◇. From above, substitute ◡ for ◆ for final answer of ◯ ◡.

Page 4: b, 3, 4

From 1st balance, substitute ★ for ▪ ◯ on 2nd balance so ▮ = ◯ ★ (Answer 3). On 3rd balance, substitute ▮ for ◯ ★ so ◯◯ ★★ = ▮▮ (Answer 4).

Page 5: d, 2, 4

From 2nd balance, substitute ⬤⬤ for ◺ on 1st balance so ⬤⬤⬤ = 6 (Answer 2) or ⬤ = 2. Divide in half so ◡ = 1. On 1st balance, substitute 2 for ⬤ so ◺ + 2 = 6 or ◺ = 4. Divide ◺ = 4 in half so ◺ = 2 and 6 (Answer 4). Therefore, ◺ ◺ ◡ = 4 + 4 + 1 = 9.

Page 6: c, 2, 4

Divide 1st balance in half so ◉ = ▪ (Answer 2). Triple so ◉◉◉ = ▪▪▪ (Answer 4) or ▪▪▪. From 2nd balance, substitute ☐ for ▪▪ so ◉◉◉ = ▪ ☐.

Page 7: b, 2, 4

Divide 1st balance into thirds so ⬭ = 4. On 2nd balance, substitute 4 for ⬭ so ◺◺ + 4 = 10. Subtract 4 from both pans so ◺◺ = 6 (Answer 2) or ◺ = 3. On 3rd balance, substitute 3 for ◺ so 3 + ◇ = 8 or ◇ = 5 (Answer 4). Therefore, 9 = 4 + 5 = ⬭ ◇.

Page 8: a, 2, 3

From 1st balance, substitute ⬭⬭ for ☆☆⬡ on 3rd balance so ▮ = ⬭⬭⬭⬭ (Answer 2). From 2nd balance, substitute ◇ for ⬭ so ▮ = ◇ ◇ = ⬭⬭⬭⬭ (Answer 3).

Page 9: d, 1, 4

On 2nd balance , remove ⬤ from both pans so ◆◆ = ◺ (Answer 1). Substitute 10 for ◺ so ◆◆ = 10 or ◆ = 5. On 1st balance, substitute 5 for ◆ so ☐☐ + 5 = 15. Subtract 5 from both pans so ☐☐ = 10 or ☐ = 5. If ☐ = 5 and ◆ = 5, then ☐ = ◆ (Answer 4) or ☐☐ = ◆◆.

Page 10: a, 2, 3

On 3rd balance, remove ▮ from both pans so ☐ = ⬤⬤ ⬤ (Answer 2). On 1st balance, substitute ⬤⬤ for ☐ so ⬤⬤⬤⬤ = ★★. Divide in half so ★ = ⬤⬤ (Answer 3). From 2nd balance, substitute ★ for ⬡ on 4th balance so ★ = ⬤⬤

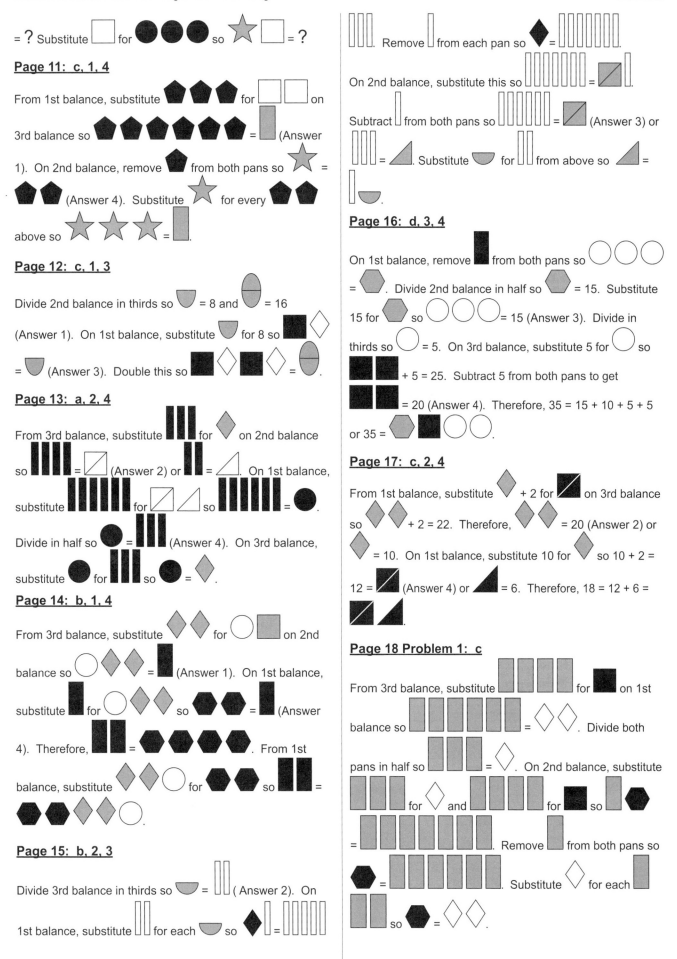

= ? Substitute ☐ for ●●● so ★☐ = ?

Page 11: c, 1, 4

From 1st balance, substitute ⬠⬠⬠ for ☐☐ on

3rd balance so ⬠⬠⬠⬠⬠ = ▮ (Answer

1). On 2nd balance, remove ⬠ from both pans so ★ =

⬠⬠ (Answer 4). Substitute ★ for every ⬠⬠ above so

★★★ = ▮.

Page 12: c, 1, 3

Divide 2nd balance in thirds so ◡ = 8 and ⬭ = 16

(Answer 1). On 1st balance, substitute ◡ for 8 so ◼◇

= ◡ (Answer 3). Double this so ◼◇◇ = ⬭.

Page 13: a, 2, 4

From 3rd balance, substitute ▮▮▮ for ◇ on 2nd balance

so ▮▮▮▮ = ◹ (Answer 2) or ▮▮ = ◺. On 1st balance,

substitute ▮▮▮▮▮▮ for ◹◺ so ▮▮▮▮▮▮ = ●.

Divide in half so ● = ▮▮▮ (Answer 4). On 3rd balance,

substitute ● for ▮▮▮ so ●● = ◇.

Page 14: b, 1, 4

From 3rd balance, substitute ◇◇ for ○▮ on 2nd

balance so ○◇◇ = ▮ (Answer 1). On 1st balance,

substitute ▮ for ○◇◇ so ◆◆ = ▮ (Answer

4). Therefore, ▮▮ = ◆◆◆◆. From 1st

balance, substitute ◇◇○ for ◆◆ so ▮▮ =

◆◆◇◇○.

Page 15: b, 2, 3

Divide 3rd balance in thirds so ◡ = ▮▮ (Answer 2). On

1st balance, substitute ▮▮ for each ◡ so ◆▮ = ▮▮▮▮▮

Page 16: d, 3, 4

On 1st balance, remove ▮ from both pans so ○○○

= ⬡. Divide 2nd balance in half so ⬡ = 15. Substitute

15 for ⬡ so ○○○ = 15 (Answer 3). Divide in

thirds so ○ = 5. On 3rd balance, substitute 5 for ○ so

◼◼ + 5 = 25. Subtract 5 from both pans to get

◼◼ = 20 (Answer 4). Therefore, 35 = 15 + 10 + 5 + 5

or 35 = ⬡◼○○.

Page 17: c, 2, 4

From 1st balance, substitute ◇ + 2 for ◸ on 3rd balance

so ◇◇ + 2 = 22. Therefore, ◇◇ = 20 (Answer 2) or

◇ = 10. On 1st balance, substitute 10 for ◇ so 10 + 2 =

12 = ◸ (Answer 4) or ◣ = 6. Therefore, 18 = 12 + 6 =

◸◣.

Page 18 Problem 1: c

From 3rd balance, substitute ▮▮▮ for ◼ on 1st

balance so ▮▮▮▮▮▮ = ◇◇. Divide both

pans in half so ▮▮▮ = ◇. On 2nd balance, substitute

▮▮▮ for ◇ and ▮ for ◼ so

= ▮▮▮▮▮▮▮▮. Remove ▮ from both pans so

⬡ = ▮▮▮▮▮. Substitute ◇ for each ▮

so ▮▮⬡ = ◇◇.

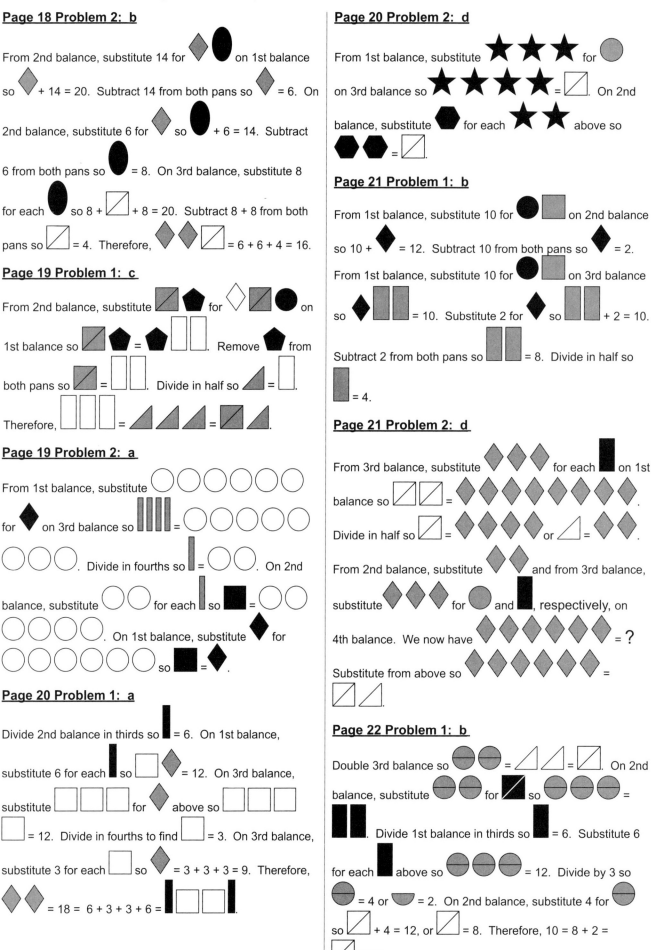

Page 18 Problem 2: b

From 2nd balance, substitute 14 for ◇⬤ on 1st balance so ◇ + 14 = 20. Subtract 14 from both pans so ◇ = 6. On 2nd balance, substitute 6 for ◇ so ⬤ + 6 = 14. Subtract 6 from both pans so ⬤ = 8. On 3rd balance, substitute 8 for each ⬤ so 8 + ◻ + 8 = 20. Subtract 8 + 8 from both pans so ◻ = 4. Therefore, ◇◇◻ = 6 + 6 + 4 = 16.

Page 19 Problem 1: c

From 2nd balance, substitute ◸⬠ for ◇◰⬤ on 1st balance so ◸⬠ = ⬠◻◻. Remove ⬠ from both pans so ◸ = ◻◻. Divide in half so ◺ = ◻. Therefore, ◻◻◻ = ◺◺◺ = ◸.

Page 19 Problem 2: a

From 1st balance, substitute ○○○○○ for ◆ on 3rd balance so ‖‖ = ○○○○○○○○. Divide in fourths so ‖ = ○○. On 2nd balance, substitute ○○ for each ‖ so ◼ = ○○○○○○○○○. On 1st balance, substitute ◆ for so ◼ = ◆.

Page 20 Problem 1: a

Divide 2nd balance in thirds so ▮ = 6. On 1st balance, substitute 6 for each ▮ so ◻◇ = 12. On 3rd balance, substitute ◻◻◻ for ◇ above so ◻◻◻ = 12. Divide in fourths to find ◻ = 3. On 3rd balance, substitute 3 for each ◻ so ◇ = 3 + 3 + 3 = 9. Therefore, ◇◇ = 18 = 6 + 3 + 3 + 6 = ▮◻◻▮.

Page 20 Problem 2: d

From 1st balance, substitute ★★★ for ○ on 3rd balance so ★★★★ = ◻. On 2nd balance, substitute ⬡ for each ★★ above so ⬡⬡ = ◻.

Page 21 Problem 1: b

From 1st balance, substitute 10 for ⬤◼ on 2nd balance so 10 + ◆ = 12. Subtract 10 from both pans so ◆ = 2. From 1st balance, substitute 10 for ⬤◼ on 3rd balance so ◆▯▯ = 10. Substitute 2 for ◆ so ▯▯ + 2 = 10. Subtract 2 from both pans so ▯▯ = 8. Divide in half so ▯ = 4.

Page 21 Problem 2: d

From 3rd balance, substitute ◇◇◇ for each ▮ on 1st balance so ◸◸ = ◇◇◇◇◇◇◇◇◇. Divide in half so ◸ = ◇◇◇◇ or ◺ = ◇◇. From 2nd balance, substitute ◇ and from 3rd balance, substitute ◇◇◇ for ○ and ▮, respectively, on 4th balance. We now have ◇◇◇◇◇ = ? Substitute from above so ◇◇◇◇◇ = ◻◺.

Page 22 Problem 1: b

Double 3rd balance so ◓◓ = ◺◺ = ◸. On 2nd balance, substitute ◓◓ for ◨ so ◓◓◓ = ◼◼. Divide 1st balance in thirds so ▮ = 6. Substitute 6 for each ▮ above so ◓◓◓ = 12. Divide by 3 so ◓ = 4 or ◖ = 2. On 2nd balance, substitute 4 for ◓ so ◻ + 4 = 12, or ◻ = 8. Therefore, 10 = 8 + 2 = ◻◖.

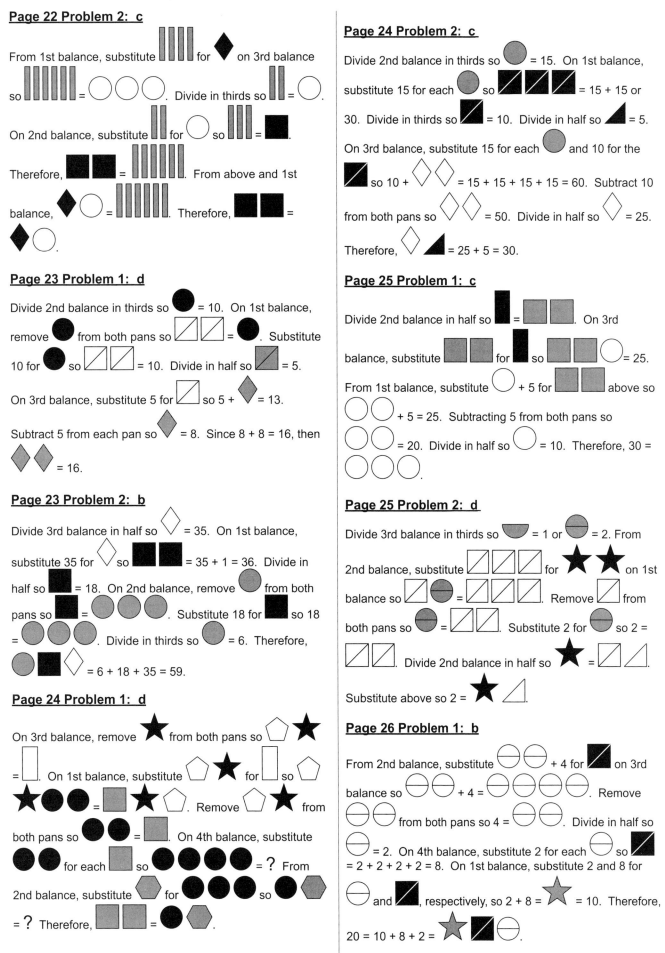

Page 22 Problem 2: c

From 1st balance, substitute ▮▮▮▮ for ◆ on 3rd balance

so ▮▮▮▮▮▮ = ◯◯◯. Divide in thirds so ▮▮ = ◯.

On 2nd balance, substitute ▮▮ for ◯ so ▮▮▮ = ■.

Therefore, ■ ■ = ▮▮▮▮▮. From above and 1st

balance, ◆ ◯ = ▮▮▮▮▮. Therefore, ■ ■ =

◆ ◯.

Page 23 Problem 1: d

Divide 2nd balance in thirds so ● = 10. On 1st balance,

remove ● from both pans so ◥◥ = ●. Substitute

10 for ● so ◥◥ = 10. Divide in half so ◥ = 5.

On 3rd balance, substitute 5 for ◥ so 5 + ◆ = 13.

Subtract 5 from each pan so ◆ = 8. Since 8 + 8 = 16, then

◆ ◆ = 16.

Page 23 Problem 2: b

Divide 3rd balance in half so ◇ = 35. On 1st balance,

substitute 35 for ◇ so ■ ■ = 35 + 1 = 36. Divide in

half so ■ = 18. On 2nd balance, remove ● from both

pans so ■ = ● ● ●. Substitute 18 for ■ so 18

= ● ● ●. Divide in thirds so ● = 6. Therefore,

● ■ ◇ = 6 + 18 + 35 = 59.

Page 24 Problem 1: d

On 3rd balance, remove ★ from both pans so ▯

= ▢. On 1st balance, substitute ⬠ ★ for ▯ so ⬠

★ ● ● = ▢ ★ ⬠. Remove ⬠ ★ from

both pans so ● ● = ▢. On 4th balance, substitute

● ● for each ▢ so ● ● ● ● = ? From

2nd balance, substitute ⬡ for ▢ so ● ● ● ● ⬡ =

? Therefore, ▢ ▢ = ● ⬡.

Page 24 Problem 2: c

Divide 2nd balance in thirds so ● = 15. On 1st balance,

substitute 15 for each ● so ◣ ◣ ◣ = 15 + 15 or

30. Divide in thirds so ◣ = 10. Divide in half so ◢ = 5.

On 3rd balance, substitute 15 for each ● and 10 for the

◣ so 10 + ◇ ◇ = 15 + 15 + 15 + 15 = 60. Subtract 10

from both pans so ◇ ◇ = 50. Divide in half so ◇ = 25.

Therefore, ◇ ◢ = 25 + 5 = 30.

Page 25 Problem 1: c

Divide 2nd balance in half so ▮ = ▢ ▢. On 3rd

balance, substitute ▢ ▢ for ▮ so ▢ ▢ ◯ = 25.

From 1st balance, substitute ◯ + 5 for ▢ ▢ above so

◯ ◯ + 5 = 25. Subtracting 5 from both pans so

◯ ◯ = 20. Divide in half so ◯ = 10. Therefore, 30 =

◯ ◯ ◯.

Page 25 Problem 2: d

Divide 3rd balance in thirds so ◗ = 1 or ● = 2. From

2nd balance, substitute ▱ ▱ ▱ for ★ ★ on 1st

balance so ▱ ● = ▱ ▱ ▱. Remove ▱ from

both pans so ● = ▱ ▱. Substitute 2 for ● so 2 =

▱ ▱. Divide 2nd balance in half so ★ = ▱ ◺.

Substitute above so 2 = ★ ◺.

Page 26 Problem 1: b

From 2nd balance, substitute ◖ ◖ + 4 for ◥ on 3rd

balance so ◖ ◖ + 4 = ◖ ◖ ◖ ◖. Remove

◖ ◖ from both pans so 4 = ◖ ◖. Divide in half so

◖ = 2. On 4th balance, substitute 2 for each ◖ so ◥

= 2 + 2 + 2 + 2 = 8. On 1st balance, substitute 2 and 8 for

◖ and ◥, respectively, so 2 + 8 = ★ = 10. Therefore,

20 = 10 + 8 + 2 = ★ ◥ ◖.

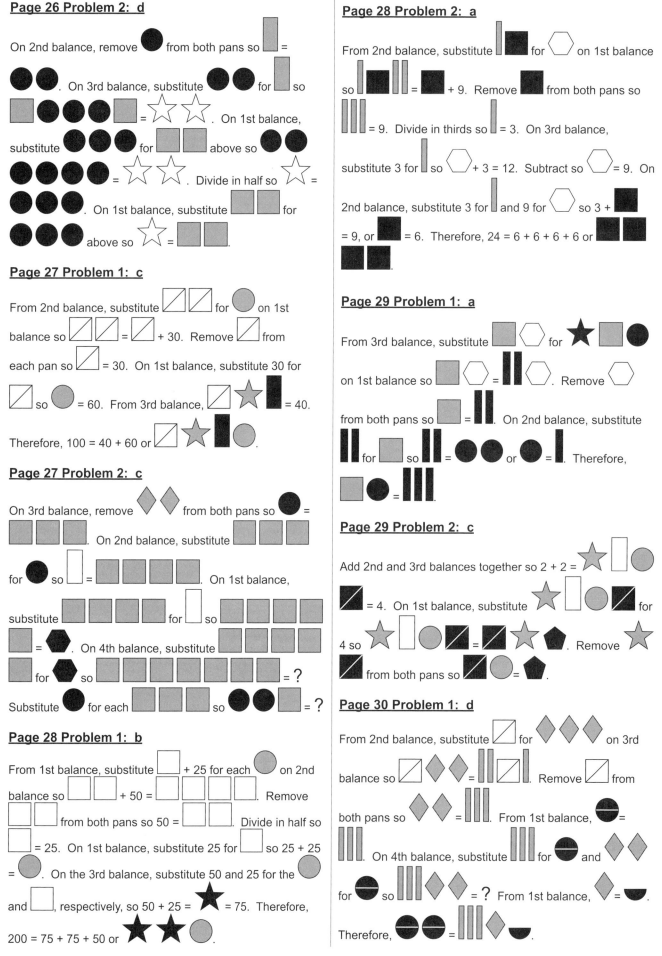

Page 26 Problem 2: d

On 2nd balance, remove ● from both pans so ▯ = ●●. On 3rd balance, substitute ●● for ▯ so ▮●●●▮ = ☆☆. On 1st balance, substitute ●●● for ▯▯ above so ●●●●●● = ☆☆. Divide in half so ☆ = ●●●. On 1st balance, substitute ▯▯ for ●●● above so ☆ = ▯▯.

Page 27 Problem 1: c

From 2nd balance, substitute ◩◩ for ◯ on 1st balance so ◩◩ = ◩ + 30. Remove ◩ from each pan so ◩ = 30. On 1st balance, substitute 30 for ◩ so ◯ = 60. From 3rd balance, ◩☆▮ = 40. Therefore, 100 = 40 + 60 or ◩☆▮◯.

Page 27 Problem 2: c

On 3rd balance, remove ◆◆ from both pans so ● = ▮▮▮. On 2nd balance, substitute ▮▮▮ for ● so ▯ = ▮▮▮▮▮▮. On 1st balance, substitute ▮▮▮▮▮▮ for ▯ so ▮▮▮▮▮▮▮▮▮ = ⬡. On 4th balance, substitute ▮▮▮▮▮▮▮▮▮ for ⬡ so ▮▮▮▮▮▮▮▮▮▮▮▮ = ? Substitute ● for each ▮ so ●●▮ = ?

Page 28 Problem 1: b

From 1st balance, substitute ▯ + 25 for each ◯ on 2nd balance so ▯▯ + 50 = ▯▯▯. Remove ▯▯ from both pans so 50 = ▯▯. Divide in half so ▯ = 25. On 1st balance, substitute 25 for ▯ so 25 + 25 = ◯. On the 3rd balance, substitute 50 and 25 for the ◯ and ▯, respectively, so 50 + 25 = ☆ = 75. Therefore, 200 = 75 + 75 + 50 or ☆☆◯.

Page 28 Problem 2: a

From 2nd balance, substitute ▮■ for ⬡ on 1st balance so ▮■▮▮ = ■ + 9. Remove ■ from both pans so ▮▮▮ = 9. Divide in thirds so ▮ = 3. On 3rd balance, substitute 3 for ▮ so ⬡ + 3 = 12. Subtract so ⬡ = 9. On 2nd balance, substitute 3 for ▮ and 9 for ⬡ so 3 + ■ = 9, or ■ = 6. Therefore, 24 = 6 + 6 + 6 + 6 or ■■■■.

Page 29 Problem 1: a

From 3rd balance, substitute ▢⬡ for ☆▢● on 1st balance so ▢⬡ = ▮▮⬡. Remove ⬡ from both pans so ▢ = ▮▮. On 2nd balance, substitute ▮▮ for ▢ so ▮▮ = ●● or ● = ▮. Therefore, ▢● = ▮▮▮.

Page 29 Problem 2: c

Add 2nd and 3rd balances together so 2 + 2 = ◪ = 4. On 1st balance, substitute ☆▯◯◪ for 4 so ☆▯◯◪ = ◪☆⬠. Remove ◪ from both pans so ☆▯◯ = ◯ = ⬠.

Page 30 Problem 1: d

From 2nd balance, substitute �diag for ◆◆◆ on 3rd balance so ◩◆◆ = ▮▮▮. Remove ◩ from both pans so ◆◆ = ▮▮▮. From 1st balance, ⊖ = ▮▮▮. On 4th balance, substitute ▮▮▮ for ⊖ and ◆◆ for so ⊖ = ▮▮▮◆ = ? From 1st balance, ◆ = ⌣. Therefore, ⊖⊖ = ▮▮▮◆⌣.

Page 30 Problem 2: c

From 1st balance, substitute 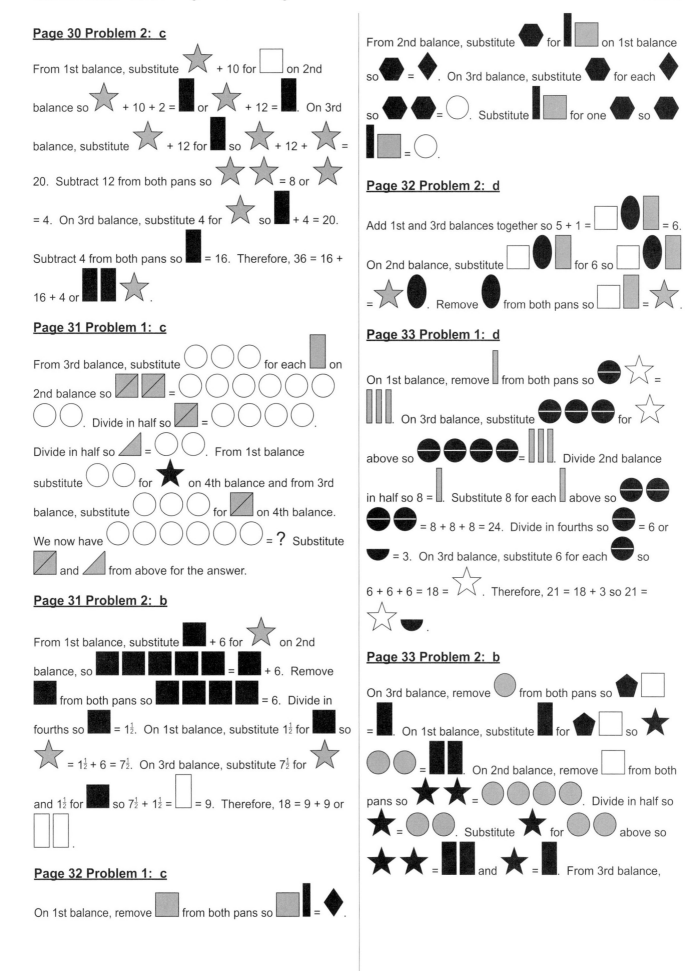 + 10 for ▢ on 2nd

balance so ★ + 10 + 2 = ▮ or ★ + 12 = ▮. On 3rd

balance, substitute ★ + 12 for ▮ so ★ + 12 + ★ =

20. Subtract 12 from both pans so ★ ★ = 8 or ★

= 4. On 3rd balance, substitute 4 for ★ so ▮ + 4 = 20.

Subtract 4 from both pans so ▮ = 16. Therefore, 36 = 16 +

16 + 4 or ▮▮★ .

Page 31 Problem 1: c

From 3rd balance, substitute ◯◯◯ for each ▮ on

2nd balance so ◨◨ = ◯◯◯◯◯◯

◯◯ . Divide in half so ◨ = ◯◯◯◯ .

Divide in half so ◸ = ◯◯ . From 1st balance

substitute ◯◯ for ★ on 4th balance and from 3rd

balance, substitute ◯◯◯ for ◨ on 4th balance.

We now have ◯◯◯◯◯◯ = ? Substitute

◨ and ◸ from above for the answer.

Page 31 Problem 2: b

From 1st balance, substitute ▮ + 6 for ★ on 2nd

balance, so ▮▮▮▮▮▮ = ▮ + 6. Remove

▮ from both pans so ▮▮▮▮ = 6. Divide in

fourths so ▮ = 1½. On 1st balance, substitute 1½ for ▮ so

★ = 1½ + 6 = 7½. On 3rd balance, substitute 7½ for ★

and 1½ for ▮ so 7½ + 1½ = ▯ = 9. Therefore, 18 = 9 + 9 or

▯▯ .

Page 32 Problem 1: c

On 1st balance, remove ▢ from both pans so ▢▮ = ◆ .

Page 32 Problem 2: (continued top right)

From 2nd balance, substitute ⬢ for ▮▢ on 1st balance

so ⬢◆ = ◆ . On 3rd balance, substitute ⬢ for each ◆

so ⬢⬢ = ◯ . Substitute ▮▢ for one ⬢ so

▮▢ = ◯ .

Page 32 Problem 2: d

Add 1st and 3rd balances together so 5 + 1 = ▢⬭▢ = 6.

On 2nd balance, substitute ▢⬭▢ for 6 so ▢⬭▢

= ★⬭ . Remove ⬭ from both pans so ▢▢ = ★ .

Page 33 Problem 1: d

On 1st balance, remove ▮ from both pans so ⬤☆ =

▮▮▮ . On 3rd balance, substitute ⬤⬤⬤ for ☆

above so ⬤⬤⬤⬤ = ▮▮▮ . Divide 2nd balance

in half so 8 = ▮. Substitute 8 for each ▮ above so

⬤⬤ = 8 + 8 + 8 = 24. Divide in fourths so ⬤ = 6 or

◗ = 3. On 3rd balance, substitute 6 for each ⬤ so

6 + 6 + 6 = 18 = ☆ . Therefore, 21 = 18 + 3 so 21 =

☆◗ .

Page 33 Problem 2: b

On 3rd balance, remove ◯ from both pans so ⬠▢

= ▮. On 1st balance, substitute ▮ for ⬠▢ so ★

◯◯ = ▮▮. On 2nd balance, remove ▢ from both

pans so ★★ = ◯◯◯◯ . Divide in half so

★ = ◯◯ . Substitute ★ for ◯◯ above so

★★ = ▮▮ and ★ = ▮. From 3rd balance,

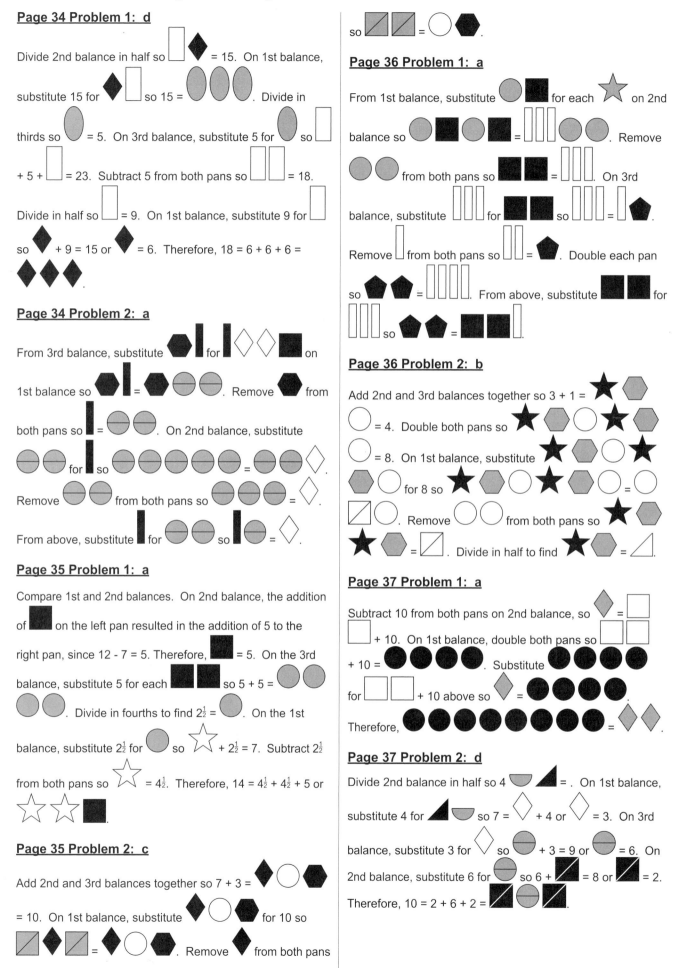

Page 34 Problem 1: d

Divide 2nd balance in half so ▭◆ = 15. On 1st balance, substitute 15 for ◆▭ so 15 = ⬭⬭⬭. Divide in thirds so ⬭ = 5. On 3rd balance, substitute 5 for ⬭ so ▭ + 5 + ▭ = 23. Subtract 5 from both pans so ▭▭ = 18. Divide in half so ▭ = 9. On 1st balance, substitute 9 for ▭ so ◆ + 9 = 15 or ◆ = 6. Therefore, 18 = 6 + 6 + 6 = ◆◆◆.

Page 34 Problem 2: a

From 3rd balance, substitute ⬣▮ for ◇◇ ▪ on 1st balance so ⬣▮ = ⬤⬤. Remove ⬣ from both pans so ▮ = ⬤⬤. On 2nd balance, substitute ⬤⬤ for ▮ so ⬤⬤⬤⬤⬤⬤ = ⬤⬤⬤ ◇. Remove ⬤⬤ from both pans so ⬤⬤⬤ = ◇. From above, substitute ▮ for ⬤⬤ so ▮⬤ = ◇.

Page 35 Problem 1: a

Compare 1st and 2nd balances. On 2nd balance, the addition of ■ on the left pan resulted in the addition of 5 to the right pan, since 12 - 7 = 5. Therefore, ■ = 5. On the 3rd balance, substitute 5 for each ■■ so 5 + 5 = ⬤⬤. Divide in fourths to find $2\frac{1}{2}$ = ⬤. On the 1st balance, substitute $2\frac{1}{2}$ for ⬤ so ☆ + $2\frac{1}{2}$ = 7. Subtract $2\frac{1}{2}$ from both pans so ☆ = $4\frac{1}{2}$. Therefore, 14 = $4\frac{1}{2}$ + $4\frac{1}{2}$ + 5 or ☆☆■.

Page 35 Problem 2: c

Add 2nd and 3rd balances together so 7 + 3 = ◆○⬡ = 10. On 1st balance, substitute ○⬡ for 10 so ◩◆◩ = ◆○⬡. Remove ◆ from both pans

so ◩◩ = ○⬡.

Page 36 Problem 1: a

From 1st balance, substitute ⬤■ for each ☆ on 2nd balance so ⬤■⬤■ = ▯▯▯⬤⬤. Remove ⬤⬤ from both pans so ■■ = ▯▯▯. On 3rd balance, substitute ▯▯▯ for ■■ so ▯▯▯ = ▯⬠. Remove ▯ from both pans so ▯▯ = ⬠. Double each pan so ■■ = ▯▯▯▯. From above, substitute ■■ for ▯▯▯ so ⬠⬠ = ■■▯.

Page 36 Problem 2: b

Add 2nd and 3rd balances together so 3 + 1 = ★⬡ ○ = 4. Double both pans so ★⬡○★⬡ = ○ = 8. On 1st balance, substitute ⬡○ for 8 so ★⬡○★⬡ = ○◹○. Remove ○○ from both pans so ★⬡ = ◹. Divide in half to find ★ = ◺.

Page 37 Problem 1: a

Subtract 10 from both pans on 2nd balance, so ◇ = ▯▯ + 10. On 1st balance, double both pans so ▯▯ + 10 = ⬤⬤⬤⬤. Substitute ⬤⬤⬤⬤ for ▯▯ + 10 above so ◇ = ⬤⬤⬤⬤. Therefore, ⬤⬤⬤⬤⬤⬤⬤⬤ = ◇◇.

Page 37 Problem 2: d

Divide 2nd balance in half so 4 ◗ = ◣. On 1st balance, substitute 4 for ◣◗ so 7 = ◇ + 4 or ◇ = 3. On 3rd balance, substitute 3 for ◇ so ⬤ + 3 = 9 or ⬤ = 6. On 2nd balance, substitute 6 for ⬤ so 6 + ◤ = 8 or ◤ = 2. Therefore, 10 = 2 + 6 + 2 = ◤⬤◤.